CELTIC

SCRAPBOOK

Written By
Michael O'Neill

sona BOOKS

First Published by Danann Media Publishing Limited 2022

CAT NO: SON0536

Photography courtesy
Getty Images

Shaun Botterill/Allsport
Allsport UK
Stu Forster /Allsport
John Chillingworth
Ullstein bild
Daily Herald/Mirrorpix

Randolph Caughie/Ian Elder/Mirrorpix
Ian MacNicol
Jay Barratt - AMA
Dave Cannon/Allsport
Craig Williamson/SNS Group
Craig Foy/SNS Group

Mark Leech/Offside
SNS Group
Aubrey Washington/SNS Group
Alan Harvey/SNS Group
Laurence Griffiths

Other images: The Press Association,Photoshot, UPPA, Talking Sport, Fotosports

Book layout & design Darren Grice at **Ctrl-d**

Copy Editor Cam Thurlow

Made in EU.
ISBN: 978-1-912918-96-6

the CONTENTS

INTRODUCTION

It is impossible to trace the exact origins of what evolved into the riveting sport known as football, the "beautiful game"; they are lost somewhere in the mists of memory that swirl around human activity as they may do on an autumn morning at Celtic Park Stadium. So we must indulge in that wonderful pastime, speculation, spiced with some good, calculated guesses.

Whenever football is mentioned, Britain will be part of the conversation before long, so it is fitting that Britain has its part in the ancient folklore of the origins of the sport.

Local legends in both Chester and Kingston-on-Thames tell us that a game was played in those towns in which the amputated head of a defeated Danish prince, or a ruffian, which probably came to the same thing, was kicked around. That seems to be a good starting point; considering the curses from the terraces that wish a similar fate would befall the top goalscorers of opposing teams in the present-day game. In Derbyshire they would have us believe that Anglo-Saxon victory celebrations against the Romans brought on the desire to kick something else, as kicking the Romans had been such fun.

Long before that, written evidence supports the claim that the Romans and Greeks were instrumental in the game's birth. They played many ball games, as the Roman writer Cicero testified. One unfortunate man was killed whilst having a shave, wrote Cicero, when a ball came hurtling into the barber's shop where he was sitting. The Romans used ball games for more serious reasons, too. They were considered a good way to sharpen a soldier's reactions and spirit for battle.

The Chinese, inventive as they have always been, seem to have been ahead of the game as well. A form of football was played in the third and second centuries BC. during the Han dynasty, when people were already rushing around and kicking leather balls into a small net or through a hole in a piece of silk cloth stretched between two poles. It was probably played for the emperor's amusement. There is no record of what happened if he got bored, and relegation would not have been much fun back then. The game, as played by Chinese aristocrats, was known as t'su chu. But the Aztecs, Persians, Vikings and Japanese all had some form of ball game for entertainment. Luckily not against one another.

It was English peasants, however, who are said to be responsible for the increasing popularity of the game sometime around the 9th century AD. This old football game was a real free-for-all, and participants were allowed to bite, punch, stab and gouge as well as kick. Not much has changed in a thousand years after all. The ball had to be taken to a certain spot, and this game proved to be so popular that fields would be overflowing with eager sports fans. As you can imagine, it often got wildly out of hand. Archers would even sneak away from archery practice to watch.

Medieval Britain was undoubtedly the place where football began its unstoppable campaign. We still have an account of a match played in 1280; it took place in Northumberland, near Ashington. It's also the first report of a player being killed, when he ran onto the dagger worn by an opposing player. There is no report as to whether the dagger was in or out of the sheath at the time!

At what point the game reached Scotland is uncertain; there is no evidence that highlanders played it, so it may be that the game was brought in by players from France or England. In Scotland as in England, the medieval game involved not only kicking the ball, but also running whilst holding the ball, and scrummages. Team numbers might bulge alarmingly, numerically overwhelming the opposition. Not so very different to the game I saw last Saturday, then.

There is a present-day link to this early version of the game that is still played today; it can be found in Scotland. It's called Ba game. Depending on where the players were born they are either 'uppies' or 'downies', and the game flows around the streets of towns in the Scottish Borders and the Orkney Isles, in Duns, Scone, or Kirwall for example, at Christmas and New Year.

Incidents of violence became so frequent, in fact, that in 1365, King Edward III banned the game altogether. The ban was also an attempt to keep his archers at their practice (yes, they were still sneaking away from work) as their skills were sorely needed following the outbreak of the black plague that had decimated the population of the country.

King James I of Scotland, too, was very upset with the ruckus the ball game caused, and went even further, declaring in 1424 that, "Na man play at the Fute-ball". Perhaps his team kept losing. Whatever the cause, his 'Football Act' of 1424 outlawed football. Not to any great effect it would seem, if subsequent bans are anything to go by.

So by medieval times Scotland was already in the grip of football fever. Even royalty were eventually won over; in 1497, the king is known to have bought footballs, although there is no note of him playing the game himself.

James V is said to have gone to Jedburgh to take part in a game, though, but that story has never been properly confirmed.

Moving along another half century, dribbling and areas marked out to contain the field of play had come into existence, as the manuscript collection of the miracles of King Henry VI of England testifies:

". . . is called by some the foot-ball game. It is one in which young men, in country sport, propel a huge ball, not by throwing it into the air but by striking it and rolling it along the ground, and that not with their hands but with their feet . . ."

Scottish writers were now documenting this rumbustious sprawl, too; Gavin Douglas, in the years between 1501 and 1512 comments that;

"This broken shin that swells and will not be relieved, take it to him; he broke it at ball, and tell him it will be his reward. Take the whole of this bruised arm to him ..."

Sir Richard Maitland (Lord Lethington), whose father fell at the Battle of Flodden, was born in 1496. He was a Scottish lawyer, poet, and collector of Scottish verse. He also wrote satirical verses, and one of them, expressing his gratefulness that he will never have to play the game, runs:

"When young men come from the green,
Having been playing football,
Their shoulders broken,
I thank my God for failing eyesight,
I am so old."

In "The Bewties of the Fute-Ball", a sixteenth century Middle Scots writer uses humour to 'praise' the game;

"Brissit brawnis and brokin banis,
Stride, discord and waistie wanis.

Crukit in eild syne halt withal,
Thir are the bewties of the fute-ball."

("Torn muscles and broken bones,
Strife, discord and devastated homes,
Crooked in old age, limping, too,
Such are the beauties of football.")

King Henry VIII reputedly bought the first pair of football boots in 1526, and by 1546, the game was becoming so popular that the Scottish Company of Hammermen, the blacksmiths, had to order that "... neither servants nor apprentices 'play football', under penalty of a pound of wax". Well, either the lads used a lot of candles or they had very hairy wives; either way, you would not want to upset them!

Football had become much more organised by then. In 1581, English schools were providing reports of "parties" or "sides", "judges over the parties", and "training masters". But although the violence had lessened, it still raised its head. In 1595 a document stated: "Gunter's son and ye Gregorys fell together ... at football. Old Gunter drew his dagger and both broke their heads, and they died both within a fortnight after."

1606 saw similar clashes in Scotland; during a "fute-ball" match at Lochtoun, reports mention that some of the players "fell in contentioun and controversie, ilk anie with otheris, and schot and dilaschit pistolettis and hacquebuttis". You certainly needed a good marksman in your squad! A couple of 'lusty' full backs who didn't shirk from "contentioun and controversie" wouldn't have gone amiss either.

By the 1600s, football was an established and increasingly popular part of Scottish life, and references to it in the literature of the day became more frequent. In 1608, Shakespeare had King Lear say, "Nor tripped neither, you base football player". This was the first time "football" had been spelt in the modern manner.

" . . . lusty shepherds try their force at football, care of victory . . . They ply their feet, and still the restless ball, toss'd to and fro, is urged by them all."

FOOT-BALL.

That was the Poet Edmund Waller (c.1624).
"The streete (in London) being full of footballs."
That was the famous diarist Samuel Pepys in 1665.

In Manchester in 1608, the local authorities complained that: "With the ffotebale . . . there hath beene greate disorder in our towne of Manchester we are told, and glasse windowes broken . . . by a companie of lewd and disordered persons using that unlawful exercise of playing with the ffotebale in ye streets of the said towne . . ."

Must have been visiting fans ...

In Scotland, Aberdeen schoolboys were now playing the game, too, apparently. It had not become any less violent and bore a great resemblance to modern rugby football. Those same Aberdeen youths incurred the disapproval of the Puritans, who accused them of profane behaviour on the Sabbath: " ... drinking, playing football ... and roving from parish to parish". The scowling was all to no avail, and even though the Puritans were less virulent in Scotland than in England, players in both countries blithely continued to enjoy the game. Here is evidence; in March 1648, Sir Patric Hume of Polwarth, Scotland, wrote to his wife.

Their son, he said, had "… hurt himself so evill at football in Polwart upon Sunday that he was not able to sturre".

Not even an act passed by the Scottish Parliament in 1656 outlawing all boisterous games on the Lord's day produced the desired effect.

Football had come so far by 1660 that a book was written about it, the first objective study of the game in Britain. The author was Francis Willoughby, and he called his work, 'The Book of Sports'. It refers to goals and pitches, (goalkeeping had already been established by this time), to scoring and selecting teams and striking balls through goals. There is also a basic sketch of a football pitch and mention that a rule had been introduced so that players could not strike their opponent higher than the ball, otherwise they often ".... break one another's shins when two meet and strike together against the ball".

Even though football was often outlawed in many areas of the country with violators threatened with imprisonment, it remained popular even amongst aristocrats. "Lord Willoughby … with so many of their servants … play'd a match at foot-ball against such a number of countrymen, where my Lord of Sunderland being busy about the ball, got a bruise in the breast".

Football was really put on the map in 1681 when King Charles II of England attended a game between the Royal Household and the servants of George Monck, 1st Duke of Albemarle. Football was here to stay.

The Scottish novelist, poet and playwright, Sir Walter Scott, 1st Baronet, was born on the 15th of August 1771. He, too, felt the need to write about this violent sport. In the Lay, he writes: "In riot, revelry, and rout, Pursued the football, play". In "foot-ball", he continues, "The victory is contested with the utmost fury, and very serious accidents have sometimes taken place in the struggle".

In the 1800s, when the working man's day lasted twelve hours or more and six days a week, the only men who had enough leisure time to indulge in football were the wealthy. Certainly in Scotland in the early years of the 19th century, the Puritan bans on the game seemed to finally have an effect.

Boys at private schools, on the other hand, were encouraged to play to develop a competitive spirit and keep themselves fit, and so the rules developed that produced the game as we know it today.

Nonetheless, there were a variety of these rules regulating the matches, until in 1848, Mr. H. de Winton and Mr. J. C. Thring called a meeting at Cambridge University with twelve representatives from other schools; their eight-hour discussions produced the first set of modern rules, the Cambridge rules.

So in the truth, we have probably been throwing and kicking anything from monkey heads to coconuts and turnips since before we could walk upright. But there are at least 3,000 years of history behind the football match of today. The millennia have passed and football, soccer,

has become one of the most exciting mass entertainments of all time.

THE SCOTTISH

Clubs dedicated solely to the sport of football were formed regularly throughout the 19th century. The London Gymnastic Society was one of the first, created in the 1850s. The first club to be referred to as a club was the "Foot-Ball Club of Edinburgh" in Scotland in the period 1821 to 1824. Great Leicestershire Cricket and Football Club existed in 1840. The staff of Guy's Hospital in London formed Guys Hospital Football Club in 1843, which claims to be the oldest known football club, whilst Sheffield Football Club, founded in 1857, is the oldest club documented as not being affiliated to a school, university or other institution. The oldest club still playing association football is Cambridge University Association Football Club, which dates from 1856 or 1857.

In Scotland, the first clubs began to be formed in the late 1860s and in the 1870s. In 1867, for example, Queen's Park Football Club was founded in Glasgow. Queen's Park is now the oldest existing football club outside England, and it was the first to be formed in Scotland. Sheffield Wednesday was also formed in 1867.

Soon, club names that are recognisable to fans today were appearing; Dumbarton (1872), Celtic (1887), Rangers (1872), Heart of Midlothian (1874), Hibernian (1875), St. Mirren (1877), Aberdeen (1881), Motherwell (1886). Dundee came to the table relatively late, in 1893.

In England, it was finally decided that a set of rules was needed to which all clubs would adhere, and in 1862, thirteen London clubs met and hammered out regulations to govern the sport. This led to the formation of the Football Association in 1863 to oversee the administration of those regulations.

No history of football would be complete if the name of Ebenezer Cobb Morley was not mentioned. He was a central figure in bringing the Football Association into being. He was a player himself and a founding member of the Football Association. As captain of his team, the Barnes Club, he proposed a governing body for the sport,

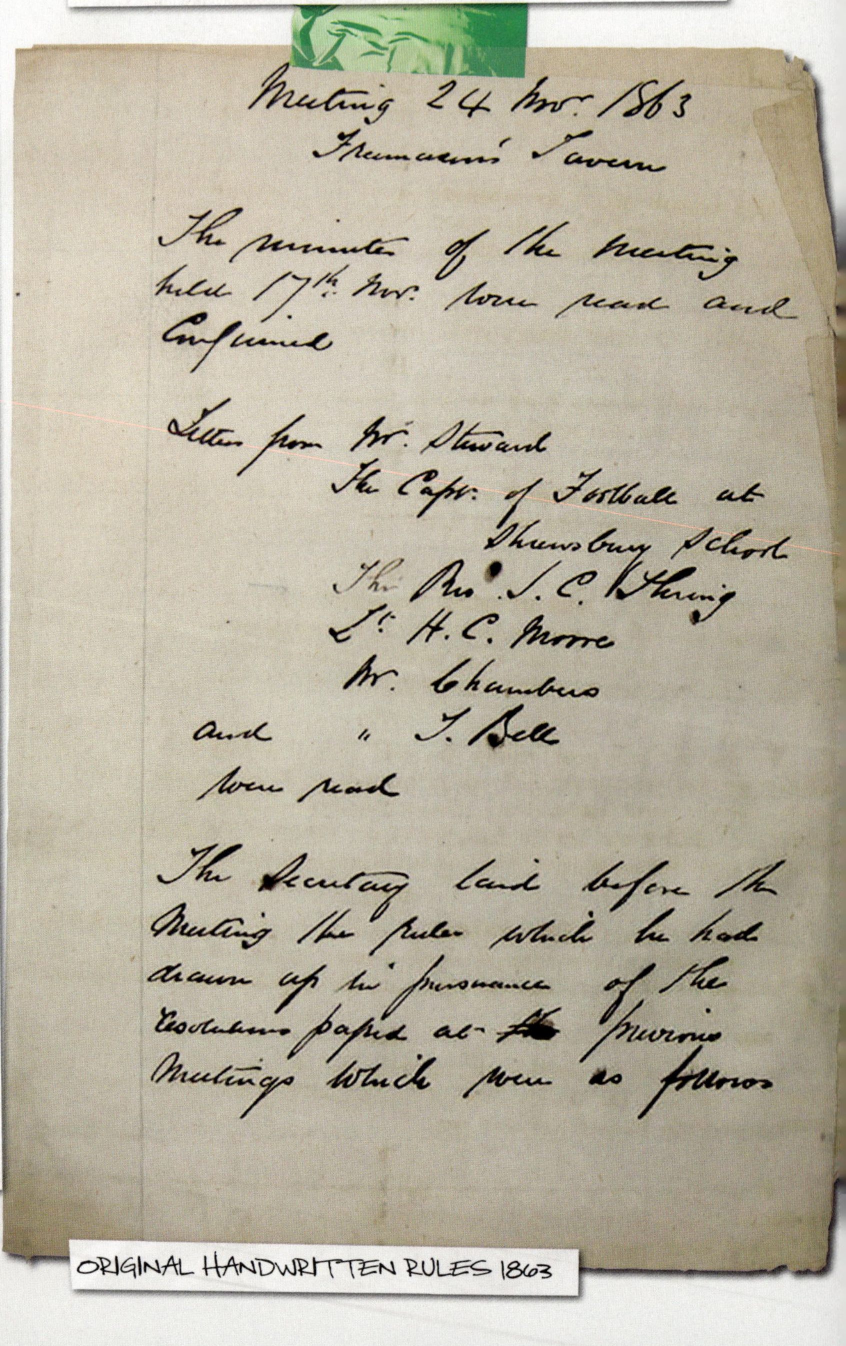
Meeting 24 Nov. 1863
Freemasons' Tavern

The minutes of the Meeting held 17th Nov. were read and Confirmed

Letter from Mr. Steward
The Capt. of Football at Shrewsbury School
The Rev. J. C. Thring
Lt. H. C. Moore
Mr. Chambers
and " J. Bell
were read

The Secretary laid before the Meeting the rules which he had drawn up in pursuance of the Resolutions passed at the previous Meetings which were as follows

ORIGINAL HANDWRITTEN RULES 1863

EBENEZER COBB MORLEY

FOOTBALL LEAGUE

and so the meeting of the thirteen London clubs came about. From 1863-1866 he was the FA's first secretary, and from 1867-1874 its second president. He drafted the "London Rules" at his home in Barnes in London.

Two momentous footballing events took place in 1873 in Scotland. Firstly, the Scottish Cup was established, and secondly, the Scottish Football Association was formed - which means that it is now the second oldest national football association in the world - when the representatives of seven Scottish clubs gathered and agreed to form an association. With Kilmarnock sending a letter of intent to join, the clubs were; Queen's Park (Glasgow), on whose initiative the meeting took place, Clydesdale, Vale of Leven, Dumbreck, Third Lanark, Eastern and Granville.

Another event must be mentioned here: the first official international game between England and Scotland took place on the 30th of November 1872 on the West of Scotland Cricket Ground in Partick, Scotland, in Glasgow's West End. 4,000 spectators watched a 0-0 draw, although the Scots had a goal disallowed. The very first game between the sides had taken place on the 5th of March 1870 at the Oval cricket ground in London. This was one of a series of four internationals. Scotland won their first international victory when they beat England 4-2 in Glasgow in 1874.

Most of the men playing in the teams at the time were amateurs, although betting had long been a feature of the sport. On the 18th of July 1885, it was finally decided that football could become a professional sport. But clubs were still setting their own fixture dates and the whole structure was chaotic. Now was the moment for another man to step into the limelight and make his mark on history; Mr. William McGregor, a director of Aston Villa Football Club. He had been raised in Scotland, in Perthshire, although for most of his life he had lived in Birmingham in England.

It was the 2nd of March 1888. McGregor wrote to the committees of several football clubs to propose a league competition that would guarantee a certain number of fixtures and bring some order into the confusion that still existed. In Anderson's Hotel in London on the 23rd of March 1888, on the eve of the FA Cup Final, a meeting was held to discuss the proposal. Manchester was once again in the headlines when on the 17th of April at the Royal Hotel, a final meeting created the Football League.

On the 8th of September 1888, twelve clubs, Accrington, Aston Villa, Blackburn Rovers, Bolton Wanderers, Burnley, Derby County, Everton, Notts County, Preston North End, Stoke, FC., West Bromwich Albion and Wolverhampton Wanderers, sent their players out onto the turf for the first games in the new Football League season.

Many Scottish players, the Scotch Professors as they were known, were moving south of the border, lured by the high salaries. So, soon after the formation of the English Football League, Peter Fairly, secretary of Renton Football Club, called a meeting of thirteen Scottish clubs. All the clubs except Queen's Park and Clyde attended. The year was 1890. On the 30th of April 1890, the Scottish Football League (SFL) was inaugurated. Celtic were present at the beginning of this historic era; together with ten other clubs they set out into that first season on the 23rd August 1890. Celtic's opponents were Abercorn, Cambuslang, Dumbarton, Heart of Midlothian, Rangers, Cowlairs, St. Mirren, Third Lanark, Vale of Leven, and Renton, who were expelled after five games for concealed professionalism… and then reinstated.

By 1893, the Scottish League had become professional anyway, and that same year a Second Division was added to accommodate the increasing number of clubs wishing to join. Many clubs came from the Scottish Alliance that had been set up in 1891.

In 1892, the English League also expanded with the addition of a new Second Division. Newcastle United joined the world of league football, as did Liverpool.

During 1898, the number of clubs in each English league increased to eighteen, and automatic promotion and relegation for two clubs was introduced the same year.

The Scottish Third Division was added in 1923, but it lasted only three years before collapsing with financial difficulties. From then on until after the Second World War, in 1946, there were only two Scottish leagues.

An English Third Division was only added after WWI, in 1921. By then, another host of well-known names, including Tottenham Hotspur and Fulham, had been added to the divisions, which by 1905 had been boosted in numbers to twenty clubs in each. There were two English third divisions, in fact; the Third Division North and the Third Division South.

With the coming of WWII, the league was suspended for seven seasons after the government banned all places of entertainment.

In post-war Scotland, there followed ten years in which the divisions were constantly renamed. The first, second and third divisions became A, B and C divisions. C division was split in 1949 to accommodate two sections; the North-West and the South-East. In 1955, there were only two divisions again, A and B, with 18 clubs in each. One year later, in 1956, divisions one and two had returned.

Over the border in England in 1950 there were twenty-four clubs in each of the two third divisions, so there were now ninety-two league clubs. The Third Division clubs were amalgamated into a single division, abolishing regionalisation, and the Fourth Division was added in 1958. Four clubs could be promoted and relegated in the lower two divisions. In divisions one and two, until 1974, two clubs made the climb, or fell; the number was increased to three that same year.

In Scotland, Division Two boasted twenty clubs in 1966 until Third Lanark left in 1967. From then until 1975 the division contained nineteen clubs. Division One operated with eighteen clubs.

In 1975 there was a major restructuring of the Scottish divisions. There were now three; Premier, First, and Second, made up of thirty-eight clubs.

A period of calm had descended on the English league system with only minor changes occurring, such as altering the points system, three instead of two for a win, a measure introduced in 1981, and goal differences being taken into account. There was one enormous change ahead, however.

On May the 27th 1992, the Premier League was formed. All First Division clubs resigned together from the Football League, which now operated with three divisions. The old system of interaction between the leagues, however, did not change, but 104 years of tradition were over. The elite clubs were now, literally, in a league of their own. Money had tempted the top clubs, and lucrative television rights deals beckoned them. Those deals will soon exceed ten billion pounds.

After a period of relative calm in Scotland that lasted for two decades, the divisions were split into four with ten clubs in each; three points would be awarded for a win.

The calm didn't last long, though, for in 1998 the Scottish Premier League was formed above the First, Second and Third Divisions. There were just ten clubs in the Scottish Premier League, which expanded to twelve in the year 2000. Forty-two clubs were now competing in the Scottish League.

And there was more adjustment to come. From 2005, there were promotion and relegation play-offs between the second, third and fourth-placed clubs in a lower division, and the club placed second from bottom in the higher division. None of the clubs that found themselves at the very foot of the Third Division, were relegated.

One more change was agreed upon. In 2013 the Scottish Football Association and the Scottish Premier League voted to merge and form the Scottish Professional Football League. The divisions are now known as; the Scottish Premiership, Scottish Championship, Scottish League One, Scottish League Two. All forty-two member clubs of the SPFL are owners of the SPFL corporation, having voting rights on a variety of issues concerning contract and rule changes.

In both Scotland, and especially England, the wealth, of course, makes it almost impossible for a promoted club to compete with the big boys in the first season after promotion. But the rewards for the successful are enormous. Clubs like Celtic are amongst the richest in the world and able to buy in players who make...

the terraces on a Saturday afternoon one of the most thrilling places to be.

IN THE BEGINNING

Without a doubt, Celtic FC owes its infancy to the fighting spirit that has subsequently brought the team to the very top echelons of the football world. That spirit was ignited in the late 1800s, a time when the people of the East End of Glasgow were undergoing terrible hardship, with poverty rife and education prospects limited - 4,750 children under the age of five died in Glasgow in 1888. And the desperate poverty was getting worse. A flame of pride rose high after the victory of an Irish football club from Edinburgh, Hibernian, in the Scottish Cup in 1887. When Hibs' secretary John McFadden uttered the words " ... go and do likewise", in his speech in Glasgow, there were several people present who were ready to pick up the torch for Glasgow's East End and do just that.

JOHN GLASS

Hot on the heels of that speech, representatives of three Glasgow parishes got their heads together to try and work out a plan for the formation of a football team. Eventually two men took over in the driving seat for the discussions, the headmasters of the Sacred Heart and St. Mary's schools, Brother Walfrid and Brother Dorotheus.

It was Sligo-born Brother Walfrid, a man admired throughout Glasgow, who proved to be the 'great persuader'. With the noble aim of helping to alleviate poverty by raising money through a football team to help one of his own charities, The Poor Children's Dinner Table, a meeting was called for the 6th November 1887. It took place in St. Mary's Hall in what was then East Rose St., Calton in Glasgow - the same hall in which John McFadden had uttered his words of encouragement - under the chairmanship of a joiner, John Glass. He was, said another Celtic legend, Willie Maley, the man to whom the club owed its existence. From then on, Glass proved to be the powerhouse behind the new club in its early years.

That historic gathering also produced a name that was to dominate Scottish football almost from the outset. That name might have been Glasgow Hibernians, a popular suggestion, but Walfrid wanted the club to be named Celtic, and his proposal was adopted. He also favoured the hard 'C' but the 'soft C' won the day. Unknown to anyone present, a legend had been born. The team gained a nickname, too; the bold boys, which eventually led to Celtic players being referred to as "The Bould Bhoys", with the 'h' indicating the Irish nature of the club, as the letters 'Bh' are commonly joined in Irish Gaelic. Unlike Hibernians, however, Celtic did not choose players exclusively according to their religious affiliations, a tradition of tolerance that the club proudly adheres to.

Two problems were solved with the same proactive determination; a piece of ground just off the Gallowgate

CELTIC TEAM 1887-88 SEASON

in Parkhead was leased within a week of the meeting. (Volunteers erected a stadium on six acres that met the standards of the age and could accommodate 1,000 in an open-air stand and banked earth terracing on the other three sides.

As far as money was concerned, Walfrid had no qualms about using the demon drink to aid his good cause, and the worldly-wise brother knew that licensing deals would provide a continuous flow of funds. With the Archbishop of Glasgow spearheading the subscription list, Celtic were set to go.

On Monday May 28th 1888, the Celtic players ran out onto the pitch for the club's first game dressed in white shirts with green collars, black shorts and emerald green socks; around 5,000 spectators watched history being made. It was an historic occasion on another count, too, because it was the first match between archrivals Celtic and their Glasgow neighbours, Rangers. The Rangers team was composed of reserves, "The Swifts", as Rangers didn't want to risk losing to a new outfit. They wouldn't have to wait long for that to happen anyway. The Celtic team for the 'friendly' match, with men drawn from Irish clubs, was;

Michael Dolan (Drumpellier) goalkeeper, Eddie Pearson (Carfin Shamrock) right-back, J. McLaughlin (Govan Whitefield) left-back

Willie Maley (Cathcart) right half-back, James Kelly (Renton) centre half-back, Phil Murray (Cambuslang

CIRCA 1890

Hibs) left half-back, Neil McCallum (Renton) outside-right, T. E. Maley (Cathcart) inside-right, John Madden (Dumbarton) centre-forward, M. Dunbar (Edinburgh Hibs) inside-left, Charlie Gorevin (Govan Whitefield) outside-left

Neil McCallum scored the first goal for Celtic in a 5-2 win over the Ibrox club. With that success under their belts, Celtic applied to join the Scottish Football Association. The first steps in the road to greatness had been made.

With a 3-3 draw against Mossend, and a 4-3 defeat against Clyde, Celtic went into the summer break.

Brother Walfrid, John Glass, and another founding member, Pat Walsh, had enlisted the services of Tom Maley, a schoolteacher who had played for Hibs, knowing that signing him, as well as star player James Kelly, Celtic's first captain, would help to lure Hibs players to Glasgow. Unknown to Brother Walfrid, his fellow organisers had offered generous expenses for Hibs players to join Celtic in August 1888; they had rightly seen the business potential of a successful club. Celtic was admitted to the Scottish Football Association on the 21st of August 1888, and the rest … is the history of dreams come true.

There was only one official competition that year for the newly-minted Celtic side; The Scottish Cup. As yet, the Scottish League had not come into existence. Nonetheless, Celtic organised a whole raft of cup and friendly matches, fifty-six in total, which took them all over England, Ireland and Scotland. It was a sign of things to come that they won seventeen of their first eighteen non-cup games. With forward Willie Groves netting eleven goals that season, the team hammered London club Corinthians 6-2, Motherwell 8-3, and Bolton Wanderers 5-1 in May 1889. The Scottish Cup run had been spectacular, too, with the team fighting its way through to the final against Third Lanark, following an 8-0 win against Cowlairs and a 9-2 demolition of Clyde, only to lose 2-1 in the final. The consolation prize was the Glasgow North Eastern Cup, which Celtic won 6-1 against Cowlairs. It was the club's first trophy; who could have dared to imagine what prestigious silverware was to follow.

Yet it was already obvious that here was a club that was not only destined to stay the course, but was a force to be reckoned with on the field of play. When the 1889-90 season got under way, the goals kept coming as they had in the first; 10-0 against Victoria Harp, 5-2 against Dundee Harp, 5-0 against Clyesdale and 6-1 against poor Cowlairs, who by now must have dreaded the games against the Bhoys. The Scottish Cup run was a short-lived affair that season. Coming up against mighty Queen's Park in the first round, Celtic held them to a draw at home only to go down 2-1 away. In May 1890, they were brought down to earth with a 4-2 defeat at home by Third Lanark, a timely reminder that they could never rest on their laurels - there had been more losses than in the previous season - but they went into the summer with a 0-2 away win against St. Mirren under their belts. All in all, a satisfying year.

The exciting news in 1890, came in April. On the 30th of the month, the Scottish Football League had been inaugurated; eleven clubs would now compete for the first league championship; Abercorn, Cambuslang, Cowlairs, Dumbarton, Heart of Midlothian, Rangers, Renton, St; Mirren, Third Lanark and Vale of Leven. Ah, yes, and Celtic, of course.

They managed to get off to a dubious start in that historic year by having four points deducted for using ineligible players. Not that the four points would have made any difference to their third position at the end of the season, because Dumbarton and Rangers were equal partners at the top with twenty-nine points each. Dumbarton had shoved Celtic out of the Scottish Cup in the sixth round, 0-3, one of just five losses that season. Nonetheless, with rousing victories, such as the 5-0 defeat of Heart of Midlothian in the first league game, and a 9-1 win against Vale of Leven, Celtic were pounding at the big boys' doors from the beginning.

The discussions about the club's future simmered on behind the scenes, but the move away from amateur status was becoming unstoppable. The arguments off the field did nothing to dampen the enthusiasm on the field, and Celtic announced in no uncertain terms that they were heading for the top. True, fans could have been excused a moment of doubt about that when the first match of the 1891-92 season was given to Heart of Midlothian 3-1.

1896 JOHN CAMPBELL IN VILLA STRIP AFTER LEAVING CELTIC

Celtic soon made up for that slip in the best way possible. By playing the best football they could. Alex McMahon spearheaded a team that put down Rangers 3-0 in the second game of the season, erased Clyde 7-2 in the third, beat champions Dumbarton in the sixth, and went on to hammer Third Lanark twice; 5-1 and 3-1. Their form finally brought them second place, just two points behind Dumbarton. But the season's absolute thrill was reserved for the cup run. Having pushed Rangers overboard in the semi-final with a decisive 5-3 victory, the team did the same thing to Queen's Park in the final, winning their first Scottish Cup with a resounding 5-1 victory. Unfortunately, anti-Irish sentiments in the press at the time were barely hidden in the journalists' remarks. Not that Celtic fans cared; their team was to prove the doubters wrong time and again.

1892 turned out to be a pivotal year in Celtic's history for another reason; the lease on the East End ground had been due to expire in November, and the landlord, succumbing, understandably perhaps, to the desire to earn money from the successful team, raised the annual rent from £50 a year to £450.

The club responded by moving elsewhere, proving that greed does not always pay.

A new ground was quickly found; a disused brickyard in Janefield Street, two hundred yards from the old ground. Michael Davitt, an Irish patriot and leading campaigner for Irish Home Rule, laid the first sod of turf, brought over from County Donegal, together with some Irish shamrock. From those inconspicuous beginnings rose a stadium that was acknowledged to be the best in Britain, boasting a grandstand that could accommodate 3,500 spectators, and a total capacity of around 40,000. It was opened on the 20th of August 1892, and Celtic finally bought the site in 1897 for £100,000. The club and its fans had found their new home.

A new and harsher breeze was beginning to waft into life at Celtic. Brother Walfrid had been transferred to London in August 1892, and it is sad to report that rather uncharitable sentiments now reigned at the club; barely had Walfrid departed before payments to The Penny Dinner Tables were stopped.

With the 1892-93 season, Celtic were about to enter new territory. It was territory reserved for the very best in football; the number one spot in the league.

The team was spearheaded by Alex 'Sandy' McMahon and John Campbell, who netted twenty-three and twenty-five goals a piece that season to put Celtic at the head of the table with twenty-nine points, one point ahead of archrivals Rangers. Not even the loss of the Scottish FA Cup, to Queen's Park, 2-1, or the loss of the last game of the season to Third Lanark, 2-5, could dampen the excitement that came with this, the historic first of many league championships. In fact, Celtic enjoyed the experience so much that they repeated it the following season.

They did so after another change had come about in Scottish football. The Scottish Football Association had introduced a Second Division into the league, so in the 1893-94 season, Celtic found themselves in the Scottish Division One.

McMahon claimed the top goal scorer spot for himself with a magnificent thirty goals in a season that started none too confidently and included – it must be said – a ghastly 5-0 defeat at the hands of Rangers in the fourth game of the season. Well, yes, and the even more ghastly loss in the Scottish FA Cup final to that same outfit. Let's quickly pass on ... the team certainly did, and although the fans' hearts were pumping when the final two games of the season were lost, Celtic still cleared the hurdle three points clear of Heart of Midlothian to top the table for the second successive year. No mean feat for the young club. But there was even better to come.

396 D MCARTHUR, CELTIC AND SCOTLAND GOALKEEPER

Another league championship came their way in 1895-96 - sandwiched in between two fallow years. For some reason Heart of Midlothian were a stumbling block again although they only finished in fourth place; they walloped Celtic 5-0 at home. Celtic had the pleasure of a 6-2 victory over Rangers and a massive 11-0 destruction of Dundee on the way to that championship. A mark of their performances was that they scored three or more goals in all their victories except three; in those they scored twice.

When Celtic came in on fourth place at the end of the 1896-97 season, it was their worst placing ever. Which tells us the high standard of football the club was playing - in more than forty years they would never fall below fifth. Four losses and four draws were responsible, with the

worst performances against Rangers that Celtic fans had seen for many a year. A 1-1 draw at home and 2-0 defeat away.

THE EARLY

Whilst fans were being treated to excitement on the pitch, off the field there were two momentous events in 1897; Celtic FC became a limited company, and before the year was out, the club finally bought the ground at Janefield Street. There had been a great deal of wrangling and bad blood during the changeover to becoming a limited company, and the ill-feeling continued long into the following century, with the owners often considered to be out of touch with the hard-working men on the ground.

Celtic came out with all guns blazing for the 1897-1898 season, and immediately shot down Hibernian 4-1. From then on there was no stopping them, and they powered through to the end of their best season ever without losing a single game. The only points they dropped were for three 0-0 draws; against Heart of Midlothian, St. Mirren, and Rangers. New signing George Allen immediately became top goal scorer with seventeen goals as Celtic headed to the top of the table to end the season with thirty-three points, ahead of Rangers on twenty-nine.

The championship opened the gates to what proved to be a pattern for Celtic teams far into the future; successive seasons of awards. Next up in a second three-year run within ten years was the Scottish Cup – the league run was less impressive; five defeats landed them in third place, twelve points behind the winners, Rangers. That situation was less depressing than it might have been, because after a terrific cup run, Celtic had gone to Hampden Park for an Old Firm final. And Rangers came off worst.

After a goalless first half, the inimitable Alex McMahon – top goal scorer for the season with twenty-one goals, his fifth time at the top – headed in the first goal for Celtic, with Hodge pushing in the late winner in a game in which Celtic were said to have "overmatched" their rivals with "determined and brilliant football". What better way to warm the Celtic fans' hearts.

As the new century approached, a buoyant Celtic team started out on what proved to be a slightly shaky season in comparison to what had gone before. It started well enough with a run of seven unbeaten games, including two games in which the back of the net was hit eight times; against Clyde, 5-0, and against Third Lanark, 3-0. After that, the team hit a sticky patch and won just four of their remaining games. (The last one was against Rangers, a 3-2 home win.) They had to be content with second place, seven points behind the leaders; which was all the more galling because they happened to be Rangers.

Despite the 'Old Firm' rivalry on the field of play, there was still room for friendship off the field as Sandy McMahon's benefit match in September 1899 proved; Rangers came along, so that the star Celtic player, known as the 'The Duke' and the 'Prince of Dribblers', would have a match worthy of his talents.

The arrival of the new century, 1900, brought with it a revival in Celtic's fortunes. In the 1st round of the Scottish FA Cup, Celtic treated their fans to a 7-1 victory against Bo'ness, which they followed up with wins against Port Glasgow Athletic and Kilmarnock.

CELTIC FOOTBALL CLUB IN 1898-1899

They arrived at Rangers for the semi-final, and the 2-2 draw led to sweet revenge at home just over one week later; a 4-0 victory. In the final in May 1900, Queen's Park could not stop the Celtic surge, and despite heroic efforts they went down 4-3. Celtic had entered a new century in grand style by lifting the Scottish Cup for the second year in succession.

The 1900's were to usher in a period of change at Celtic. Willie Maley, Celtic's first manager, had altered the club's policy of buying in professional players, in favour of recruiting youngsters that he could mould into a team. This was a brave decision that would prove spectacularly successful; initially, though, the club would have to weather a three-year trophy drought. Many doubters in the club would have felt that they been proven correct when the team failed to reach the Scottish Cup final three years in a row, and could only finish second in the league in 1901 and 1902. Then, after a very indifferent season, they dropped to fifth in 1903, their worst final placing since joining the league in 1890. At least there had been the Exhibition Cup, won in 1901, to cheer about.

Another event that fanned the flames of doubt was Sandy McMahon's decision to leave the club that year. He moved on to Partick Thistle, retiring a year later. But his departure made way for another Celtic player to rise to stardom; forward James Quinn. He and Celtic were about to prove the doubters very wrong, and turn himself and Willie Maley into legends. There was one last change to be made before Celtic set out on the adventure that would see them dominate Scottish football for years to come; out went the vertical stripes that had accompanied them for the first years of their existence. Instead, the team that ran onto the pitch for the match against Partick Thistle on the 15th of August 1903, wore shirts bearing green and white hoops. A little bit of history had been made.

There were now fourteen clubs competing in the Scottish Division One. The new Celtic team was finding

YEARS

CELTIC TEAM, 1905-1906 SEASON

its feet, and bounced along between first and fifth positions in the 1903-04 season. They might lose at home to Third Lanark, 1-3, or wallop Kilmarnock 6-1, and then draw with Rangers at home 2-2. The best aspect of the league performance was finishing level with Rangers on 38 points, in third place. To cap it all, the north stand burned down in May. Not the best of seasons.

Once again it was the Scottish FA Cup where the excitement was to be found. Having made hard work of the qualifying rounds, Celtic found themselves in the final against Rangers. In the 1902 cup final, the team had lost to Hibernian by a single goal. This time the opposition was even fiercer, and following their performances in the league, no one was betting on the outcome.

It was a bleak first half for Celtic, who found themselves two goals down after forty-five minutes. But when they came out onto the pitch again, it was the Celtic fans who had reason to celebrate. As they gradually got into their stride, the forwards' play became what "The Scotsman" described as, "dashing". And the most dashing of all was Jimmy Quinn - top Celtic goal scorer that season for the first time for eight consecutive years - who whipped in a hat-trick that sent Celtic off the pitch as cup winners once more. It was the start of a wonderful run for the club; the team would go on to win a trophy every year until the start of the First World War, except in 1907 and 1913. They would win the double twice, in 1908 and in 1914.

With Jimmy Quinn, Alexander Bennett, and James McMenemy firing on all cylinders upfront, the 1904-05 season looked more hopeful for Celtic in the league. There were to be only three losses; against Heart of Midlothian, 0-2, Airdrieonians, 2-3, and Dundee, 1-2. The goals came thick and fast, starting with a 5-0 win away against Partick Thistle and ending with another away win, this time against Motherwell, 6-2.

By the end of the season, Celtic had lost the Scottish FA Cup to Rangers, 2-0, but were sitting on top of the league, where they had been since their 3-0 victory against Dundee in October of the previous year. Unfortunately, so were Rangers as both had 41 points. A play-off was scheduled.

The teams lined up on the 6th of May 1905, and this time Celtic kept their nerve after a close-fought game, to go two up through McMenemy and Hamilton in the 60th and 61st minutes, before Rangers pulled one back. It was not enough for the Ibrox side, and Celtic took the title. Celebrations were tinged with slight discord; it had been a sad indication of the increasingly fraught behaviour between the supporters that a neutral referee from England had had to be brought up to Scotland to oversee the match.

Whatever the supporters were up to, however, the team were on top form; they would bring home the honours every year until 1912. In 1905-06, they hit first-place on the 1st of January 1906 in a 1-0 win against Rangers, and stayed there to end the season as champions once more. Then came the historic first double, in the 1906-07 season. Celtic were the first Scottish club to achieve this difficult feat, and have repeated it fourteen more times since then. Heart of Midlothian went down in the Scottish Cup final 3-0, and one month later in May 1907, the team were league champions. They ended the season more with a whimper than a roar as the last two games ended in two draws, but they still gained 55 points to Dundee's 48.

Celtic repeated this display the following year – including the 55 points in the league, and taking draws from the final two games of the season – and became the first team to bring home both the Scottish Cup and the League Championship in successive seasons; an astonishing achievement.

Even more startling was the fact that they almost did it again in 1908-09. They made the league theirs with a one point lead over Dundee, securing the top place in the last game of the season with a 2-1 win away at Hamilton Academical.

By that time there had been another historic event.

Historic for the wrong reason.

Celtic had forged their way through to the Scottish Cup Final, where they met Rangers on May 10th 1909. The match had fans on the edge of their seats, and ended in a 2-2 draw. So far so good. When full-time ended in the replay on the 17th of May, the scores stood at 1-1. The SFA rules excluded extra time except for a second replay, although it seems that some of the players, and certainly the supporters, expected extra time to be played. When it was made clear that this was not going to happen, fans began to pour onto the pitch, and were soon engaged in a full-scale riot with the police. The riots continued outside the ground, and both clubs later stated that they did not want another replay, so the medals and cup were not awarded. There was no doubt that Celtic had missed a third double by a whisker.

CELTIC TEAM, 1907-1908 SEASON

No one could take away their next extraordinary 'first'. It arrived with the end of the 1909-10 season. The Scottish Cup would go elsewhere after Celtic's 3-1 defeat to Clyde in the semi-final. In the League, however, Celtic had been riding high since the beginning, and had only lost the top spot on five occasions early in the season. They looked to be home and dry after winning their match against Aberdeen 2-0, and with just three games left to go. But fans were left gasping after a 2-0 defeat to Falkirk was followed by two 0-0 draws against Hibernian and Dundee. Luckily, Falkirk couldn't make up the points difference, and landed on second place, two points behind Celtic on 54.

For Celtic, it had been the most remarkable decade imaginable, a decade in which they had produced consistently vivid football that had led them to an incredible title-winning run; six successive League Championships, with two Scottish Cups as well. This 'six in a row', was marked by the Scottish League with a special shield carrying the names of all the Celtic players involved.

As the team moved into the century's second decade, the players that had formed that epoch-defining side were already dispersing. Alec Bennett had moved to Rangers in 1908, the same year that William Orr retired, and Peter Somers left to play for Hamilton in 1910. By 1911, Jimmy Hay had also gone.

Three other legendary Jimmy's, Young, Quinn and McMenemy, would stay on for several more years; Quinn would be top goal scorer in 1910-11 and again in 1912-13, and McMenemy would take that honour in the 1911-12 season. All three players would see Celtic lift the Scottish Cup again in 1911 and 1912 to end what can only be described as an astonishing run of award-winning seasons; four Scottish Cups and six League Championships in ten years.

The golden era ended in 1913; Celtic missed out on the league title to Rangers, and fell to Heart of Midlothian in round four of the Scottish Cup, 0-1. It was also the end of an era in another way; Celtic's Jimmy Quinn had been top goal scorer for the club in eight successive seasons. A record, of course. He was top goal scorer again in 1913 for the last time.

There was, however, one celebration to enjoy; in June 1913, Willie Maley's Silver Jubilee arrived. No one can deny that the man who had spent 25 years at Celtic as a player, secretary and manager, and taken the club to the very top of Scottish football, remains one of the greatest names in football history.

Celtic strode out into the 1913-14 season making it clear that they would once again be vying for the honours. They lost just three league games that season, and powered their way to the top of the table. They dispensed with all their opponents in the Scottish Cup and lifted the trophy on the 16th of May 1914 winning the final 4-1 against Hibernian. Then, as if to prove that the previous season had been just a temporary aberration, they romped home to win the League Championship with 65 points, ahead of Rangers on 59, having beaten the Ibrox team twice; 4-0 and 2-0. It had been another wonderful season, crowned with a third Double.

CELTIC TEAM, 1908

During the summer, however, everyone in Scotland was worried about one thing only; was there going to be war in Europe?

As the 1914-15 season got under way, the players' thoughts, and indeed, their fans thoughts, were across the English Channel because by the time that Celtic ran onto the field to play Heart of Midlothian on the 15th of August 1914, Britain had declared war on Germany. The declaration had come on August the 4th 1914. One month later, British soldiers had begun fighting the Battle of the Marne.

The war was not over by Christmas as everyone had confidently predicted. As the weeks and months passed, players and spectators donned army kit, left Glasgow far behind, and joined tens of thousands who were being sent to the front lines in the new year of 1915 to fight on the killing fields of France. They were volunteers; conscription did not begin until 1916.

Two 'Football Battalions', The 17th and 23rd Battalions of the Middlesex Regiment (1st and 2nd Football Battalions), the 'Die-Hards', had been formed by William Joynson-Hick, MP for Brentford, in December 1914. Many of the men, of course, never returned from the battlefields of France. Nine Bradford City players lost their lives. More than 8,000 officers and men went with the Football Battalions into some of the hardest battles of the war. The soldiers were former players from many of the clubs. Professional footballers were exempt from enlistment, but on the 25th of November 1914, eleven Heart of Midlothian players signed up for service, with two others signing up on the following day.

Here are just a few of the names of Scottish men who fought and died for their country.

Robert Craig was a former Celtic player, who became a private in the 5th Battalion of the South Wales Borderers. His death came on the 19th of April 1918 from injuries sustained during the recapture of Mesen in Belgium.

Peter Johnstone was a member of the 6th Battalion of the Seaforth Highlanders. He was killed on May the 16th 1917 during the Battle of Arras; his regiment were ordered to capture a chemical factory, and during the two days of battle he was reported as missing. His death was confirmed on June 6th 1917.

Patrick Slavin was a former Celtic player; he was a sergeant with the 2nd Battalion Royal Scots. He was killed on November the 13th 1916 in the 2nd Battle for the village of Serre. Reports stated that he was shot dead after "going over the top".

John McLaughlin played for Mossend, Hibs and Renton. He joined the 11th Battalion of the Highland Light Infantry. On the 23rd of April 1917 he was injured during the Battle of Calvary Farm at Monchy Le Preux to the north of Arras. McLaughlin died from his injuries on May the 10th 1917.

Donald McLeod was another Celtic player. He joined the 466th Battery of the 65th Royal Field Artillery as a gunner. On the 6th of October 1917, McLeod died from injuries, probably in Belgium, possibly in the Battle of Passchendaele.

Archie McMillan was a Celtic player and a private in the 1st/7th Argyll and Sutherland Highlanders. McMillan was shot and killed whilst serving with his regiment during fierce fighting in the Battle of Cambrai in November 1917.

Jimmy Speirs played for Rangers, Clyde and Leeds City. Having enlisted in the Queen's Own Cameron Highlanders, despite being officially exempted, the Scotsman won a Military Medal for bravery in May 1917. He was killed in action that same year.

Sandy Turnbull played for Manchester City and Manchester United, and enlisted in 1915. Turnbull was a lance sergeant in the Eight Battalion of the East Surrey Regiment. He died in battle at Arras on May the 3rd, 1917; his body was never found.

And of course there is the inspiring story of Celtic

man William Angus, who won the Victoria Cross for gallantry in the war. The Lance Corporal left his trench during heavy bombardment and gunfire at Givenchy-lès-la-Bassée in France to save the life of a soldier who had been injured. Hit forty times, Angus lost his left eye and part of his foot in the heroic action, but survived the war. He was the first professional footballer to receive the award.

Seven former Celtic players died in the war.

Although the Scottish Division Two and the Scottish Cup were abandoned because of the outbreak of war, the First Division season continued, but under a very heavy cloud. Players' wages were reduced.

At Celtic, several men joined up immediately, while the others worked in the factories and engaged in other necessary wartime work before conscription began in 1916.

In 1914-15, there were twenty clubs in the Scottish Division One. Celtic were vying for the top spot for most of the season, taking over at number one just three matches before the end of the season to win the League.

By the time the war ended, Celtic had won the League title four times.

But life at Celtic had changed; Brother Walfrid had died on the 17th of April 1915 aged 74, Chairman James Kelly had handed over the reins to the lawyer Tom White, a member of the board since 1906. Some of the players had not returned from France, and the pre-war team greats were aging. Young players such as Tommy McInally arrived, and in turn became the new stars at Celtic Park. McInally, despite his problems with discipline, is considered to have been

one of the most magical players to have ever played at Celtic.

A SLIGHT

At the end of the 1918-19 season – a season in which Celtic lost just two games – the club once again lifted the League title with 58 points, just one point clear of Rangers. A great start to post-war football.

The twenties were proving to be less favourable to a Celtic team used to success than everyone had hoped. Links with the great past were becoming fewer, too; James McMenemy was no longer in the team.
So, Rangers were the team to beat in the 1921-22 season, and Celtic played with a sense of purpose from the beginning and lost just two games. Even though they were unable to beat Rangers on the football field, taking two draws, 0-0 and 1-1, away from their meetings, they eventually won the race to the top of the table, winning the league title with 67 points to Rangers' 66.

On the 10th of June 1922, a player joined Celtic at the beginning of a career on and off the pitch that would make Celtic fans' hearts blaze with pride; his name was Jimmy McGrory. As he made his debut in January 1923 and was loaned out to Clydebank for most of the 1923-24 season, his real talent only became apparent at Celtic when he ran out to play at the beginning of the 1924-25 season, one that will live forever in Celtic hearts.

Having returned to their winning ways in the league, Celtic decided not to bother again in the 1922-23 season. Well, that's the way it must have looked to the fans as they watched their team bounce lackadaisically between fifth and ninth positions for most of the season, to finally end on third place behind Rangers and Airdrieonians. Even though Joseph Cassidy had put away 34 goals for the Bhoys. With eleven defeats, it had been the worst season the team had ever endured. Unfortunately, there was an even worse year still to come.

Late in 1922 had come news of a tragedy that touched everyone in the club; former Celtic star James Young was killed in a motorcycle accident on the 4th of September, while riding in his native Ayrshire. The vibrant Young had played at right-half for the team and won six Scottish Cups and nine league championships with them. His career had ended following a knee injury in 1916. He was just 40 years old when he died.

Oddly, Celtic sparkled in their Scottish Cup run and made their way through the rounds without a stumble, knocking out Motherwell 2-0 in the semi-final to meet Hibernian in the final. In a game that was dominated by the defences, and although Hibernian seemed to have the best of play in the first half, it was Celtic's Cassidy who scored the deciding goal in the second half to give Celtic the cup for the tenth time.

That uneven season was followed by another damp squib. The team struggled in the first half of the season, and were ignominiously knocked out of the Scottish Cup by Kilmarnock in round one, 2-0. Ending the season in third place, therefore, even though they were thirteen points behind league champions Rangers, seemed like a good result.

Fortunately, the 1924-25 season provided such a memorable highlight and such a memorable player

that everything that had happened in the league was forgotten. Just as well, because the team and fans had to endure the worst number of defeats they had ever suffered, defeats that not even the goal feasts, 7-0 against Third Lanark, or 6-1 against Falkirk could make up for; there were twelve in total. And yes, two of those were against Rangers.

Ah, but who will ever forget what happened in the Scottish Cup? Out of a sea of indifferent performances in their round four replays (there were three of them) Celtic pulled out one of their most magical performances. And they reserved this display of football goals for Rangers.

It was the 21st of March 1925, and Celtic and Rangers met in the semi-final of the Scottish Cup. 100,000 supporters crowded into Hampden Park. Rangers had not won the cup since 1905, but were favourites to win this match.

Rangers began well, so that for twenty minutes the Celtic team were on the receiving end. But the Ibrox side couldn't capitalise on their advantage, and the McGrory legend was about to be cemented into place when he latched onto a cross by Connelly and put Celtic one up. In the second half, McLean put in the second followed by another from McGrory six minutes later. Thomson and Maclean fired in two more, and the demolition of Rangers was complete. 5-0 the final score.

After that spectacular success, the final delivered even more drama. Celtic left Hampden Park on April the 11th with the Scottish Cup in their hands having beaten Dundee 2-1. Fans also had a wonderful, once-in-a-lifetime goal by Celtic's Patsy Gallacher to savour, so that the game would always be remembered as the Patsy Gallacher Cup Final. It had been a game of two halves; the first half belonging to Dundee and the second to Celtic although the Bhoys were one goal down with just seven minutes to go. When Gallacher was brought down in front of goal after a tackle, he still had the ball between his feet and neatly somersaulted himself into the goal with the ball. It had to be seen to be believed. That piece of football magic brought the scores level, and McGrory headed in the winner just before full time. Celtic had won one of the most exciting matches all year to lift the Scottish Cup once more. McGrory was top goal scorer that season with 31 goals. Before his career ended in December 1937, he would claim that status twelve times. For McGrory, the good times were just beginning, whereas Gallacher would only appear four more times the following season, his last with the club.

All seemed well in the 1925-26 season. McGrory was firing on all cylinders, top scorer with 48 goals, and the results were good once a hiccup in September was out of the way; that had brought in three defeats in five games, including an almighty 5-1 smacking at the feet of Airdrieonians which dropped Celtic to sixth place in the league. From the end of October they began to climb back to the top, so that by the middle of November they were ahead of the pack, scraped a win from the revenge battle against Airdrieonians, 3-2, and did not relinquish their hold on the number one spot despite two more defeats. They finished the season in great style with a 6-2 home win against Dundee United. The league title was theirs and Rangers were nowhere in sight.

Against expectations, the Bhoys had allowed the historic third Double to slip through their fingers when they met St. Mirren in the Cup Final. Having beaten the club twice in the league, 2-0 away and 6-1 at home, perhaps the team was guilty of complacency.

Whatever the reason for the 2-0 defeat the opportunity was thrown away.

SLIP

THE ELUSIVE

If Celtic fans could have gazed into a crystal ball, they would not have liked what they saw prophesied for the years between 1926 and 1935, for not one league title would appear there. In fact the decade to come would be one of scarcity compared with what had gone before; Celtic fans would have to get used to the snakes as well as the ladders.

Nonetheless, the team was strong, so there seemed little to worry about as the 1926-27 season started, and yet it became a struggle to get into a position to challenge for the title again. And this time Rangers were not to be denied their glory. Double defeats for Celtic at both Rangers and Hibernian did not augur well in a season that threw up ten lost games. It was unjust that McGrory, who scored five goals on three occasions that season and set a Celtic record of 57 goals in total, should come away empty handed. He missed the Scottish Cup Final against East Fife. In that game, Celtic gave their fans an almighty fright, allowing the Fife team to go one ahead before retrieving the initiative and whacking home the equaliser less than one minute later. They won comfortably, 3-1, thanks to Paddy Connolly, McLean and an own goal from Robertson. In the newspapers the Celtic play was described as "delightful". It was an historic match for two reasons; East Fife were the first team from the Second Division to take part in the final for thirty years and it was the first Cup Final to be broadcast live on radio.

Celtic could never get their league form to gel sufficiently, and having won just four of the final eleven games they came in on third place behind Motherwell and Rangers.

Still, one highlight that year was the signing of an eighteen year-old goalkeeper; John Thomson was described by Celtic chairman Desmond White as the best goalkeeper he had ever seen. He certainly served Celtic well until 1931 when fate decreed that he had played enough. Those whom the gods love die young ... but that sad story will come soon enough.

INTERNATIONAL CITY GAME IN BERLIN BETWEEN A MIXED TEAM FROM PRUSSIA BERLIN / NORTH-NORTHWEST BERLIN AGAINST CELTIC, 1922

Celtic had not played three seasons without any honours since 1901. Now, they not only had to endure that starvation again, they had to watch Rangers take the honours every year. It was not the easiest of times for the club. Perhaps the absence of Willie Maley through illness that season, 1927-28, was significant, but of those three forlorn years the first was undoubtedly the worst, for Celtic lost both the league and the cup to their Glasgow rivals. They fought hard in the league, and clawed their way up only to stumble at the end and

win just one of the last five games, coming home second. And then the cup; after sailing through to the final, they collapsed against Rangers 4-1 to give the Ibrox team their first cup in twenty-five years. And if fans had known that the club was trying to sell McGrory to Arsenal there might have been riots, especially as the forward had achieved a personal best of 63 goals that season. McGrory of Arsenal just never sounded as good as McGrory of Celtic, quipped the player later. Thank heavens it didn't!

Anyway, it had been a season for the club to put behind them as quickly as possible.

It was an unsettled team that began the 1928-29 season; it seemed symbolic that the mercurial Thomas McInally was sold that year, and that in March 1929 the Grant stand caught fire; the fire on the field kept going out. In the middle of September Celtic began a run of eleven games with only three victories and took the rest of the season to crawl back up to second place, where they finished the season on fifty-one points, six points behind Rangers. They got through to the semi-final of the Scottish Cup, only to be knocked out 1-0 by Kilmarnock. Captain Willie McStay moved on to Hearts and was replaced as captain by his brother, James. John McFarlane also moved on.

In Celtic's case, the adage "it never rains but it pours" turned out to be true. Their form degenerated from indifferent in November 1929 to bad in December when a run of seven games brought in just one victory; against Clyde away from home, 3-2. They recovered well from that bad spell, but by the time they lost to Clyde at home in the last game of the season, 0-2, they were still only on fourth place. Their cup challenge had also disintegrated, in February in round three against St. Mirren with a 1-3 defeat. Neither was there a Glasgow Cup or Glasgow Charity Cup as a consolation prize, because Rangers had completely cleared the board that year. It was not a good place to be whilst staring out into a new decade.

CHAMPIONSHIP

This bitter pill, however, had once again been sweetened by a famous victory in the Scottish Cup against Motherwell.

Celtic were 2-0 down with just eight minutes left in the game when McGrory struck to bring back a weak spark of hope in the Celtic fans. Unbelievably, an own goal from Motherwell defender Alan Craig forced a replay. This time the team made no mistake, pushing in four goals to Motherwell's two. On that day, it seemed to every Celtic heart that the team were poised for greatness once again.

Not quite, as it turned out.

In fact, what followed was a fruitless season that started off with an appalling tragedy.

When the club looked back over the twenties, it had certainly not been their greatest run in the league; but they had at least won the Scottish Cup three times. And who could be truly downhearted with one of the greatest footballers of his age in the team, Jimmy McGrory. Nonetheless, the thirties would provide more than their fair share of disappointments for the Glasgow Bhoys.

But at least they got off to an exciting start.

The league in 1930-31 became a three-legged race between Celtic, Rangers and Motherwell. It proved to be rather inconsistent for Celtic, and although there were flashes of brilliance, 5-1 against Partick Thistle, 6-2, against Ayr United, ten drawn matches sealed Celtic's fate, handing the league title to Rangers once more by just two points.

With five wins and two draws from the first seven matches, everything seemed to be going well in the 1931-32 season, and everyone was looking forward to the match against Rangers on the 5th of September.

When the teams parted at half-time, no goals had been scored. As the second half got underway, Rangers player, Sam English, struck at the ball in front of the Celtic goal. The young Celtic goalkeeper, John Thomson, who had given his fans such breathtaking displays of balance, and indeed beauty, whose bravery was already the stuff of legend, went for the ball. His head collided with English's knee. Thomson stayed down and was then stretchered from the field, with many unaware of the severity of the injuries; they proved to be fatal. His skull had been fractured to a depth of two inches. After a major convulsion at 5pm, an operation failed to save his life, and the young man considered to be one of the finest goalkeepers in the country, the "Prince of Goalkeepers", died at 9.25 that night. He was twenty-two years old.

"They never die who live in the hearts they leave behind." The epitaph on John Thomson's grave is certainly true in his case. Even today, many people visit his grave, and the city and club where his illustrious career began still remember him.

The Celtic team went on to a lacklustre season by their standards, in which the Scottish Cup challenge vanished against Motherwell in round three, 0-2, and they were unable to recover from a bad patch of seven matches lost out of ten that began in February. They ended the season third in the table.

1930 JIMMY MCGRORY IN ACTION

CELTIC GOALKEEPER JOHN THOMSON DIVES AT THE FEET OF RANGERS' SAM ENGLISH, HE LATER DIED FROM THE COLLISION, 05 SEPTEMBER, 1931

In May 1933, they finished in fourth place after losing the last game to Dundee 0-3, and fans could have been forgiven for wondering if their Bhoys would ever capture the league title again.

They did, however, manage to capture the Scottish Cup fairly regularly - no mean feat - and 1933 proved to be one of those occasions. Those cup victories kept hope alive when doubts about new young players rose - this year had seen Johnny Crum, Bobby Hogg, Malcolm MacDonald, and Hugh and Frank O'Donnell, don the green and white hoops. In 1933, Celtic had to beat Motherwell, and beat them they did with a single goal from Jimmy McGrory. It was Celtic's thirteenth Scottish Cup victory. An impressive tally from any angle.

It was a triumph that had to be savoured for two years, because neither the cup nor the league came Celtic's way again until 1936.

Third place was the best that could be managed in 1934 after eleven drawn matches; not until 1980 would a Celtic team match that total again. The following season, everyone was eager to see how the new Bhoy, the young outside-right, James Delaney, who had signed on provisional terms in 1933, would fare in the first team. Unfortunately for him, the side got off to a terrible start with just three wins in thirteen games, and only a winning run over nine consecutive games enabled the team to pull back from twelfth place to second. That instant revival has been credited to the arrival of Jimmy McMenemy, who came back to Celtic to take over as Willie Maley's assistant and first team coach. Celtic's first.

Maley and McMenemy soon instigated a cull amongst the older players, as they began to rejuvenate the team – Peter McGonagle, Charles Napier and Francis and Hugh O'Donnell left the club, and Willie Lyon arrived at centre-half. Many felt that this was too much tinkering, and at the wrong time. So there was no great optimism when the 1935-36 season began. At least McGrory was still there to lead the charge.

Bringing home a 1-3 loss from Aberdeen in the first match of the 1935-36 season did nothing to calm anyone's nerves; quite the opposite.

And then, suddenly, everything went right, and the Celtic magic that had beguiled fans in the past, floated through Celtic Park. 18 games without defeat followed, as title challengers Heart of Midlothian and Motherwell fell before the Celtic surge. There were goals aplenty: 6-0 against Third Lanark, 5-3 against Dunfermline Athletic, and two successive 5-0 victories against Hibernian and then Arbroath. This was the football of champions, and so it proved to be – best to ignore the limp exit from the Scottish Cup in the second round with a 2-1 loss to St Johnstone. With the last of their four defeats that season behind them, Celtic powered back to the top of the league table in February, slamming in thirty-eight goals in their last eleven matches. This included a seventh hat-trick in the game against Ayr United for McGrory to take the league title from Rangers. McGrory notched up a second personal best of 50 goals this season, setting a new Celtic and Scottish record of 351 goals at the top level in September 1935. Truly one of the all-time greats.

1930 JOHN THOMSON, DIED AFTER COLLISION WITH RANGERS PLAYER SAM ENGLISH IN 1931

It was certainly too early to assume that Celtic had returned permanently to their trophy-winning ways. But in the short term at least, it certainly looked that way. An unbeaten run of 15 matches that started in September 1936 began the true chase for the title. But inexplicably, in December 1936, the Celtic engine began to run out of steam and brought home just seven wins in seventeen matches. It even had to endure the agony of an 8-0 drubbing by Motherwell in the last game of the season. That defeat was away from home, however, and as Celtic had taken on and beaten Aberdeen 2-1 in the final of the Scottish Cup just six days previously, the atmosphere at Celtic as the summer break arrived was still euphoric. And another record had fallen before a mighty Celtic team; 146,433 spectators had crowded into Hampton Park for that final; a record for a British club match that remains unbeaten to this day.

There was only one thing to be sad about, had anyone known about it: that season proved to be the pinnacle of Jimmy McGrory's career at Celtic. Twenty-seven goals meant that he was again top goal scorer, a position he had held at the club twelve times in thirteen years, an astonishing record matched by no other player before or since.

McGrory played just eleven matches after the new season started in the autumn of 1937, scoring six goals before bringing down the curtain on an unparalleled career in December 1937. McGrory was offered the managership of Kilmarnock, which he accepted.

1937-38 SEASON TEAM

McGrory left a team that was well and truly into its stride in the league, and which had started out on a run of twenty-games without defeat. That run saw Kilmarnock completely crushed, 8-0, Heart of Midlothian, that season's runners-up, taught a lesson 4-2, and Rangers silenced 3-0 at Celtic Park. Celtic hit the top spot in December, which seemed a fitting tribute to the departing Jimmy McGrory, and stayed there to become league champions again for the second time in three years, making a grand total of nineteen league triumphs. Yes, it had been disappointing to suffer a third round exit to Kilmarnock, 1-2, in the Scottish Cup, but that had happened seven weeks earlier, and by the time the Bhoys had claimed the league title, that pain had subsided somewhat. And there was something else to celebrate, after all; 50 years of Celtic Football Club, 50 years of excitement and glory since the club had been formally constituted by Brother Walfrid on the 6th of November 1887.

There was also the Empire Exhibition that took place in May 1938 to bring a sense of cheer to a country apprehensive about the aggressive movement of armies in Europe for the second time in just under twenty-five years.
Celtic, Rangers, Aberdeen and Hearts took their places in a football competition arranged for the event, against English clubs Everton, Brentford and Chelsea. Celtic worked their way through to the final against Everton, and on the 10th of June, in front of 82,000 spectators, the favourites Everton were taken into extra time by the Scottish club. With excitement at the Ibrox stadium intense, it was Johnny Crum who fired home the goal seven minutes into extra time that helped Celtic bring home the Exhibition Trophy. All of this gave rise to great anticipation for the 1938-39 season.

Celtic's hopes for further glory were dashed, however, by a run of five games early in the new year in which four were lost and one was drawn. That enabled Rangers to open up an unassailable lead and they finished the season on 59 points, eleven points clear of Celtic, a harsh result for a team that had dished out a 6-2 football lesson in an Old Firm clash early in the season.

The Scottish Cup dream had vanished at Motherwell in a 1-3, round four defeat, too. When Delaney was hustled to the ground in a home game against Arbroath in April 1939, the player suffered a broken arm. Arbroath player, Attilio Becchi, then accidentally stepped on Delaney's arm and Delaney was out of football for over two years. That blighted the atmosphere at Celtic Park even more, and an extremely disappointing season petered out with a loss at St. Mirren, 2-1.

When Celtic ran out onto the pitch at Aberdeen on August the 12th, 1939, no one at the ground, or anywhere else in the country, was in any doubt that the threat of war in Europe was real. Celtic played their last league game on the 2nd of September, a 1-0 victory against Clyde.

On the 3rd of September, war was declared against Nazi Germany. The mass slaughter was going to start all over again.

The Scottish League and the Scottish Cup were suspended, so there would only be regional football in Scotland for the duration of the war. As the "Phoney War" with Germany began, Celtic began to float in a state of limbo, taking no great interest in their Western Division games.

In this unreal atmosphere, the Celtic directors decided to part company with Willie Maley, who after 52 years of involvement in the club was 71 years of age. Following a meeting in February 1940, Maley 'retired'; but it was an acrimonious departure. Maley felt deeply hurt at being, in effect, pushed out, and his anger manifested itself in an unseemly row about tax payments on his golden handshake. The incident reflected well on no one, and was especially unfortunate as it took place in 1940, exactly fifty years since Celtic had joined the Scottish League in 1890. Maley had supervised the ups and downs of a club that was second to none during his extraordinary reign which had begun in 1897.

Jimmy McStay took over at Celtic Park. He was manager for five years, but had he known that even before his appointment, Jimmy McGrory was the man the directors really wanted in the manager's seat.

On May the 10th, Hitler invaded France.

Once again, Celtic players and supporters would change into battle gear. They were among countless other footballers and spectators who fought, many of whom gave their lives, to conquer a ruthless dictatorship. Because of their sacrifice and that of their fellow citizens,

football was able to continue in freedom after the war.

THE JIMMY

On the 8th of May 1945, the fighting in WWII was over. The Scottish League and the Scottish Cup competitions only restarted in August 1946, however.

On May the 9th, 1945, Celtic won a one-off football tournament, the Victory in Europe Cup, beating Motherwell in a game that had to be decided on the number of corner kicks; Celtic won the game by one. It was at least a good omen for the future.

In July 1945, the Celtic board asked Jimmy McStay to resign so that they could bring in the man they had always wanted to manage Celtic: Jimmy McGrory. Reluctantly, McStay left the club.

In that final season before normal competitions began, the Scottish First Division had become the Scottish League A Division. McGrory's first year in charge saw Celtic come home in fourth place. That performance gave no clue as to what was to happen next.

It was a different Celtic team that ran out onto the field on August the 31st 1946 than the one that had competed in the League before the war. There was no John Crum, no James Delaney, no Charles Geatons, no James Kennaway, no Malcolm MacDonald. Neither was there any sparkle in a team that won just one game in its first nine outings that season. At one point in September they hit sixteenth position, before recovering to pull themselves back into seventh position by the end of the season. It was the worst result for a Celtic team in the history of the club. To make matters worse, there had been a swift exit in the Scottish Cup in round one against Dundee when Celtic lost 2-1. Neither did they qualify for the new Scottish League Cup competition. McGrory, it seemed, was not the man to bring back glory to Celtic Park. No one had any swift solutions; it was a bleak time at Celtic Park.

EVANS OF CELTIC (LEFT) AND COX OF GLASGOW RANGERS COMPETE FOR THE BALL DURING A DERBY MATCH AT IBROX STADIUM.

Behind the scenes, Chairman Tom Whitehead died on March 4, 1947, and in his place came Robert Kelly who had been a director at the club since 1931. Kelly became the dominant force at Celtic, and his presence was such that the question, did Jimmy McGrory have any influence at all, would never go away during the manager's tenure. Later, in the fifties, Sean Fallon would say, "Bob Kelly was the boss. He was always responsible for picking the team." Which seemed to be a quite definite statement on which way the wind blew.

1947 had been a bad year, but 1948 was even worse. Celtic collapsed in the league and lost fifteen matches; their worst result ever, which saw the team only just scrap north of relegation. The Scottish Cup was lost, although they had reached the semi-final, where they went down to Morton, 1-0. They had failed to qualify for the League Cup for the second year running.

The club signed Jock Weir early in the season, and never had there been a more vital purchase at Celtic Park. Not knowing who was going to go down on the final day of the season, Celtic's away game against Dundee became a game of life and death. Especially for Jimmy McGrory, who was set to resign should Celtic lose the match. It was a contest that only a Celtic supporter with nerves of steel could have endured. There were two disallowed Celtic goals netted by John McPhail, then a Jock Weir goal for Celtic and then a goal for Dundee just before the interval. In the second half, it seemed as though Dundee had plunged in the knife when they took the lead, only for Celtic's Jock Weir to put the scores level. It was Weir again, who finally saved the club with a hat-trick, 3-2 the final score, and Celtic were safe. It had been the most awful experience anyone could remember. Surely there would have to be drastic action if the club was to be saved from oblivion?

The directors were aware they had to act quickly, but when they did, the decisions hardly seemed ground-breaking. Star player Charles Tully came from Belfast Celtic, and Jimmy Hogan was hired as first team coach. Hogan had been coach with the England national team for six years; his appointment was the smartest move the board made that year, and he was credited with the improvement in form that took away the immediate threat of relegation in the 1948-49 season. Tully needed a few games to get into his stride, but he was soon working his way into the hearts of the Celtic faithful.

The team were joint sixth with Third Lanark when the final whistle blew in May 1949, having suffered eleven defeats, been beaten 3-4 by Dundee in round one of the cup and by Rangers 2-1 in the League Cup. A sigh of relief all round for a very average year in Celtic terms. For a team that could boast the combined talents of Charlie Tully, Bertie Peacock, Sean Fallon and Bobby Collins, it really wasn't good enough.

In a sign of how dramatically Celtic had fallen, it was a good result in 1949-50 when they came in on fifth place at the end of the season having lost 'only' nine games. The Scottish Cup challenge was over in round three and the League Cup attempt failed in the first round. Jimmy Hogan reached the end of his two-year contract, which sent shivers through everyone; were the good times over forever?

MCGRORY ERA

There was little to inspire confidence that they would return soon. John McPhail had equalled Jackie Gallacher's previous season top score of 21 goals, and he now set out into the fifties to claim that spot again in 1951 with 30 goals. One glimmer of hope flickered in March 1950. A future Celtic legend arrived, and played in the last game of the season; Sligo-born Sean Fallon. Fallon would go on to gain eight caps with the Republic of Ireland team, and despite being offered highly unfavourable terms at Celtic, he signed up. Fallon had weighty personal reasons for doing so, apart from Celtic's reputation - which was still hanging on by its fingernails. Jimmy McMenemy had saved Fallon's sister from drowning in Lough Gill in Ireland. McMenemy later sent Fallon a Celtic shirt and a book, "The Story of Celtic" by Willie Maley. Fallon was hooked. There were other changes; George Hunter would be between the posts in place of Willie Miller, who had been at the club since 1942.

From a less than catastrophic start, Celtic slumped in January 1951 to nine defeats in twelve matches; it seemed as though they were in a free fall that would never end. That they landed on seventh spot seemed miraculous. So did the fact that they managed to lift themselves out of the first round of the League Cup for the first time. For the record, they then fell to Motherwell, 2-4 on aggregate after the second leg of the quarter-finals. That was in September 1950. In April 1951 they met Motherwell again, by which time an even greater miracle had occurred; Celtic had downed Heart of Midlothian 2-1 and Aberdeen 3-0, both of whom finished higher up the table than Celtic, and were set to meet Motherwell in the Scottish Cup final.

Who cared that the game was "disappointing" as The Times put it. What mattered was that McPhail was on target in the twelfth minute, and that goal gave Celtic the cup. Their first since 1937.

In goal, George Hunter had been man of the match, 134,000 spectators watching his "brilliant" performance. The Times reported that his handling and clearing were "magnificent". Against all expectations, Celtic were back.

Not for long, sadly.

Celtic set off on an exhausting but exciting tour of America in the summer. When they returned, the Festival of Britain was well under way, and Celtic entered the St. Mungo Cup competition, initiated by Glasgow Corporation to be part of the celebrations. Sixteen clubs competed, and Celtic found themselves in a second final that year, coming up against Aberdeen. After 35 minutes, Celtic were two goals behind, and as the second half began it seemed that the task ahead was too great for the Glasgow men.

Until Charles Tully and Sean Fallon set the stadium alight and the Celtic fans home happy with four goals, two each after great play between them. It was a terrific way to make fans look forward to another season in Division A.

In autumn 1951, Celtic won just two of their first ten games, and fans were right if they thought that this was not going to be the season to record that Celtic made a thrilling comeback. Twelve defeats saw to that.

Not even a momentous event in December that no one realised would change Celtic profoundly and magnificently, changed the run of horrible results. December was the month that Jock Stein arrived. Along with centre half Bobby Evans and defender Bertie Peacock, Stein would form one of the greatest triumvirates ever seen at Celtic Park. As a player he would be at the club until 1957, but it was his return in 1965 as the Bhoys' manager that would set Celtic on a path of blazing glory …

But we have to get through the agony years first before that story can be told.

Let's pass swiftly over the 1951-52 and 1952-53 seasons because they were saturated with unfulfilled hopes. Ninth place in April 1952 was followed by eighth in April 1953 and not even a glimpse of a major cup. There were two highlights in 1953; the first was delivered by Charlie Tully in the third round of the Scottish Cup tie at Falkirk. His corner kick two minutes into the second half, sailed in an arc towards the goal and landed in the back of the net. It was disallowed, perhaps because Charlie had not set the ball down inside the marked area. He had to retake it. Incredibly, the ball sailed in an arc towards the goal and landed in the back of the net for a second time. An extraordinary achievement that set off a frenzy of cheering amongst Celtic supporters.

The second highlight was the Coronation Cup competition held to commemorate Queen Elizabeth's coronation in May 1953. It proved that Celtic could beat the best, as they amazed everyone, probably including themselves, and kicked out Arsenal and Manchester United, to beat high-flying Hibernian in the final, 2-0. If only they could repeat those performances there would be a bright future. Jock Stein was captain of that team, incidentally.

No one was prepared for the events of the 1953–54 season.

It started out in what had become a familiar manner; a 2-0 loss at Hamilton Academical. After that, the team settled into one of their best seasons for many a year, until the 2-3 loss to Heart of Midlothian on the 6th of February 1954, that is.

From that point on, the team didn't miss a beat, and set out on a nine-game winning run that brought them to the end of the season and the final home game against a team who had beaten them in the first game of the season: Hamilton Academical. This time Celtic took the honours with a 1-0 victory. That was reason enough for the fans to cheer themselves hoarse: their team had won the Scottish league championship with 43 points, five points ahead of second-placed Heart of Midlothian. Suddenly, the world had turned on its head at Celtic Park, because two days earlier, on the 24th of April 1954,

JOCK STEIN OF CELTIC 7TH OCTOBER 1953

Celtic had beaten Aberdeen 2-1 in the final of the Scottish Cup. The Bhoys had come from nowhere to win their third Double, the first since 1914. It was a terrific season for Neil Mochan, too, who was often used at whatever position needed to be strengthened. He became top goal scorer with 22 goals, and would take the honours in two further seasons. It is pleasing to record that this most trustworthy of Celtic players, who joined the team in 1953 and stayed with them until 1960, would have a blazing hour of glory with the team. Three years would pass before that happened, but what an hour it was to be!

During the entire 1954-55 season, Celtic pressed hard to take the top spot in the league. They produced bushels of scintillating performances against the top contenders, Aberdeen, Hibernian, Rangers and Heart of Midlothian. They started off with a terrific 2-0 win against Rangers and repeated the score against Aberdeen to take over the number one spot in November. But it was a hard-fought season, and although Collins, Willie Fernie, Neil Mochan, Tully, Peacock and Jimmy Walsh had glittering treats up their sleeves for the fans in nearly every match – 6-3 against Kilmarnock, 7-0 against Stirling Albion, 5-0 against Hibernian, 5-2 against St. Mirren and 3-0 against Heart of Midlothian were some of the best scores – they simply could not reclaim the championship, and finished three points behind Aberdeen, who were champions with 49 points.

Similarly, disappointment awaited them in the Scottish Cup, where Celtic had pushed impressively through to the final against Clyde. The first match ended in a draw; 1-1, but the replay went to Clyde by a single goal. As usual, the Scottish League Cup competition was unkind with Celtic third in their qualifying group.

There were highlights to be found in the 1955-56 season when the number of clubs competing in Division A was increased to 18; you had to be lucky to find them, however. The 3-2 against Hibernian away from home was one of them. But it was also fun to hammer Falkirk 5-1 in the Scottish League Cup. The true highlight came on the 27th of August 1955 in a superb 4-1 victory over Rangers at Ibrox. It was a magnificent performance by the Celtic team that left Rangers breathless. Billy McPhail scored with a fierce shot after 16 minutes, and this was followed with another 12 minutes later when Neil Mochan passed for Eric Smith to score. Rangers' only piece of luck was an own goal by Sean Fallon, which was quickly revenged when Eric Smith powered in his second to make it 3-1 at half-time. When Mochan thundered home the fourth goal after 52 minutes, fans could hardly contain themselves.

The awful inconsistency that bedevilled the Celtic lineup of this time, however, meant that they went down 4-0 to Rangers at home just four days later, and said goodbye to any hopes in the Scottish League Cup competition.

On the bright side, they had managed to get through to the Scottish Cup final. Chairman Bob Kelly had reshuffled the team, as he had done so often in the past, and probably upset the fine-tuning needed to win matches. Celtic dreams were crushed by three goals from Heart of Midlothian to which they could only reply with one. The dismal season had ended with a fifth place in the league and a consolation prize in the shape of the Glasgow Cup from October 1955, which had, satisfyingly, been won at Rangers' expense, 5-3 in the replay.

What, then did the 1956-57 season have to offer to unsettled fans?

Good news ... and bad; perhaps we'll tackle the bad news first to get it out of the way, even though the good new came first.

The league; bad to mediocre is the best that can be said about it. Celtic chalked up eleven losses and were fifteenth at one point. They recovered from that low, but could never get above fifth, which is where they were when the season ended with a dismal 0-0 draw at home against Queen of the South ... who finished sixteenth in the table! So, not a great league season, as the top goal scorer John McPhail's tally of 18 goals shows.

High time for some good news.

Rangers were beaten 2-0 in a Scottish FA Cup replay after a 4-4 draw. Certainly good news; it was Celtic's first victory at Ibrox in the Scottish Cup since 1908. There was more good news with Celtic's defeat of Rangers in the Scottish League Cup, 2-1, followed with a 0-0 draw in the second leg. That result was significant for the really good news that season, because Celtic went on to the League Cup final against Partick Thistle. This was the first time that Celtic had got anywhere near the League Cup final, and the League Cup had been initiated after the Second World War, so

There had been awful news from the dressing room, too; Jock Stein had injured his ankle in a friendly match in Coleraine in Northern Ireland in May 1956, and the injury had required an operation. At the beginning of 1957, his ankle had stiffened to the point where he had to declare that his playing career was over. He officially retired on the 29th of January 1957 and took over the job of coaching the Celtic reserves, with great success.

Nor was the news from the Scottish Cup much better. In the semi-final, Celtic were knocked out by Kilmarnock in the replay, 3-1.

21ST OCTOBER 1957 LEAGUE CUP FINAL, HAMPDEN PARK, RANGERS' GOALKEEPER GEORGE NIVEN MAKES A SPECTACULAR SAVE. CELTIC WON 7-1

into the second half, McPhail put Celtic ahead, and three minutes later they were two up when a McPhail shot hit the back of the net after beautiful teamwork by Tully and Mochan. Bobby Collins was on target twelve minutes later and Celtic had deservedly won their first League Cup trophy.

The second one came the very next season. The Celtic surge in that competition became unstoppable during the autumn of 1957, with East Fife going down 4-1 and 6-1, Third Lanark going down 6-1 and 3-0, and Clyde going down 4-2 in the semi-final.

There was now only one team between Celtic and their second consecutive League Cup Trophy: holders of the league title, Rangers.

Rangers had already succumbed to Celtic in September at Celtic Park, 3-2, so the match had the potential to be a real cracker. And it fulfilled and surpassed every expectation that the Celtic Park fans had. It became a match to remember forever.

On the 19th of October 1957, Celtic ran out onto Hampden Park on a sunny afternoon that lead to the match being dubbed, Hampden in the Sun, towards a famous victory. Three of the best players in Scotland were in that team; Peacock, Tully and Evans, and this final was to be one game that they would never forget.

It was Celtic's day from the start, and within twenty minutes they had struck Rangers' goal posts twice. Then, on the 23rd minute, ecstasy, as Wilson headed in a Charlie Tully cross, to give Celtic a deserved lead, which was wiped out just five minutes later when Simpson scored for Rangers.

Had the fans worried that this was going to mean the end of Celtic, they couldn't have been more wrong. Mochan put the Celtic Park club back in the lead at the end of the first half.

And then Rangers' worst nightmare came true; Celtic rampaged through their defence. McPhail gave himself a hat-trick with a header, and Mochan, who dominated Rangers' right-back, Shearer, throughout the match, gave himself a second goal. With a penalty awarded at the end of the game, Fernie put the nail in Rangers' coffin, to make the final score an incredible 7-1. It was another Celtic record; a record score for the final of a major competition.

What a match! What a team!

What of the league?

Well, the snakes and ladders nature of the Celtic seasons was about to make itself felt with a vengeance when the league games began in the autumn of 1957. Supporters and players would have to live on the heady fumes of that League Cup final for a long time, because the endurance of even hardened fans would soon be put to a severe test.

The league challenge started out well enough; eleven matches without defeat. And then came the kind of stumble that fans knew only too well. It came in December 1957, a four-match run without a win that ended on the 1st of January 1958 with a defeat at the hands of Rangers at Celtic Park 1-0. Injuries to Fernie and McPhail, Tully and Collins hadn't helped. Despite notching up a host of good wins after that, 4-0 against Hibernian, 5-1 against Queens's Park, 6-2 against Clyde, the Bhoys couldn't make up the difference again, and ended the season in third place with 46 points, three behind Rangers. In the Scottish FA Cup, the dream had vanished with a 2-0 defeat to Clyde in round three.

From that point on, fans would be subjected to another drought; there would be no more trophies for six years.

They were years of change; many of the stars were ageing, and their glory days at Celtic were behind them. Sean Fallon ended his days as a player when he suffered an injury during the summer. Bobby Collins requested a transfer in August 1958, and the unique and legendary talents of Charlie Tully were lost when he retired early in 1959 after eleven years and 319

RANGERS GOALKEEPER BILLY RITCHIE IS ON THE GROUND AND CELTIC'S NEIL MOCHAN HAS AN OPEN GOAL UNTIL WILLIE TELFER (LEFT) CAME TO RANGERS' RESCUE AT PARKHEAD IN GLASGOW ON 1ST JANUARY 1958.

appearances. Keeper Dick Beattie was replaced by Frank Haffey that season. Before the drought ended Bertie Peacock and Bobby Evans would also have gone.

1958-59 was a season in which Celtic won only twice against the top five teams and rolled home on sixth place, well behind the league leaders, Rangers.

Another new decade broke, 1959-60, with Celtic less than scintillating. They lost thirteen games in the league, their worst result ever, and they could only manage two drawn games against Stirling Albion, who were relegated; they dropped to ninth at the final whistle in April. 1960 was also the year when Celtic reached their fourth consecutive Scottish Cup final, losing again: 4-1 to Rangers in a replay following a 1-1 draw. 1960 was also the year Jock Stein left. 1960 was the year that Celtic were finally forced to adopt numbered shirts, which became compulsory that year. 1960 was a low point for everyone at the club. It was also a year of a Rangers resurgence.

Hope dared raise its head the following year. After three defeats in the first five games had come and gone, that is. And another three defeats in six games in a run that started in November. It was a fairly painful crawl back up the table, which ended on fourth place with 39 points; well behind league champions Rangers on 51. That crawl had included an awful 5-1 defeat to Rangers, a 6-1 victory against Hibernian, a 6-1 victory against Clyde, and a defeat in the Scottish Cup final against Jock Stein's Dunfermline Athletic in the replay, 0-2, plus another loss to Rangers in the Scottish League Cup 2-1 at home, following a 3-2 victory at Ibrox.

Players were now earning £26 a week, a rise intended to act as a counterweight to the charms of England, where the maximum wage had been abolished. That enabled the club to retain the services of its promising young players, such as Billy McNeill, Paddy Crerand and Bertie Auld, and acquire the services of a hugely talented youngster named Jimmy Johnstone.

Celtic's failure to get to the top continued into the 1961-62 season when they were third in the league, and into 1962-63 when they were fourth. Some writers put it down to the lack of bite and discipline in the attack as it approached the opposition goal. Perhaps, though, the solution to the problems, was off the field of play, but no one was yet taking it seriously; the dead weight of the chairman on every decision and its timing – Kelly could prevent a player knowing that he was in the team until ten minutes before a match started. And a change of manager was needed.

At least there had been a first that season; the club was in a European competition for the first time. They were knocked out in the first round of the Inter-Cities Fairs Cup, 4-6 on aggregate to Valencia, but a start had been made that was to bear rich fruit very shortly. Glory almost came in the Scottish FA Cup, but vanished in the final during the replay after three goals from Rangers. Another bitter day for everyone involved the club.

Resentment against Kelly was increasing, and supporters began to protest by staying away. The club desperately needed new blood, experienced heads on the field to guide the talented youngsters, and fresh thinking off the field. How would that come about with the all-powerful chairman as immovable as a boulder?

There was no change for the start of the 1963-64 season; no change by the end of it either. In seven games the team scored five or more goals – nine against Airdrieonians – proving that there was no lack of talent, and they lost just six games in total, two of those against Rangers. That season's highlight, without doubt, took place in Europe again; Celtic beat their way through to the semi-final of the European Cup Winner's Cup only to lose 4-3 on aggregate against MTK Budapest. At least a glimpse of things to come, hopefully. Centre-forward Stevie Chalmers took the honours as top goal scorer that year with an impressive forty goals. Chalmers would eventually become the fourth highest goal scorer for the club

1960 CELTIC'S JOHN CLARK PASSES THE BALL AS TERRY VENABLES AND JIMMY GREAVES OF TOTTENHAM LOOK ON

with 231 goals in 406 appearances. This was his second year as top goal scorer and the Celtic stalwart would take that honour again for the third time the following season.

By now, the rumblings of discontent could be heard loud and clear on the terraces and in the boardroom. Celtic were so far off the running, said the press, that there was not even a contest between the Old Firm sides.

When the first games of 1964-65 got underway, Bertie Auld was back in the ranks. Frank Haffey wasn't, and Billy McNeill was teetering on the brink of leaving, and almost succumbed to the siren lure of other more successful clubs. Who could have known what was about to happen that eventful year would change the club's future so dramatically.

Celtic's league form soon had them bobbing around six and even seven places below the top clubs; but although there was inconsistency in the League Cup competition, a mighty 6-0 walloping of East Fife revived hope of better things to come. And indeed, the team were soon in the final against Rangers. Celtic lost 2-1, yet the narrow margin of the defeat was a boon against the dominant club for several seasons past. Disappointment, then, especially as they lost to Kilmarnock horribly, 2-5, the week after in the league and went down to sixth place. By early December, Barcelona had pushed them out of the Inter-Cities Fairs Cup, 1-3 on aggregate, so everything was lined up for another year of dissatisfaction and let down. What hope for the Scottish Cup that began in February?

3-0 away from home against St. Mirren. At least that. Another 1-0 against Queen's Park away from home. 3-2 against Kilmarnock at home. This was better. At this point Kelly made probably the best decision of his life. The pressure for change was now immense, and in March 1965 with Celtic languishing on sixth place in the league, Jock Stein arrived at Celtic Park to take over as the new manager. Celtic were about to undergo a transformation the like of which they had never known before.

Not that the ship could be turned around in one night, of course. But when the Scottish Cup semi-final was won against Motherwell, 3-0 in the replay, Stein was already pulling the strings. So against all the odds, there was a Scottish Cup final against Dunfermline to look forward to, Jock Stein's former protégées.

In a cracking match – the 80th Scottish Cup – Celtic were 2-1 down at half-time, and no team had ever recovered in that competition from being behind twice. On 52 minutes, Celtic drew level again with a second goal from Auld, and the tension became unbearable. Until McNeil headed in the winner in the dying minutes of the game to send fans into an ecstatic roar. Celtic had won 3-2 to lift the trophy. Their first senior trophy since 1957. At last; the Bhoys were not has-beens after all. But were they truly a team that could win consistently? The team to bring back the glory days?

Four days later, Dunfermline whacked them 5-1 in the final match of the season … just to remind them that one win does not make a team. Celtic finished eighth in the table.

That cup win made all the difference, though. Without it, Stein may not have been able to impose his will on his interfering chairman, Kelly, and thus set the direction for the future. With the trophy to point to, he was allowed to take charge of his team fully,

and Celtic were about to rocket to the stars.

25TH OCTOBER 1965 CAPTAIN BILLY MCNEILL AND JOHN HUGHES WITH THE SCOTTISH CUP AFTER BEATING RANGERS 2-1 AT HAMPDEN PARK

JOCK STEIN'S BHOYS

29TH SEPTEMBER 1965 JOCK STEIN DURING THE EUROPA CUP II MATCH BETWEEN GO AHEAD EAGLES AND CELTIC, DEVENTER, HOLLAND

The journey began the very next season.

Twenty-five year old Joe McBride had come along for the ride of his life. He ended his first season as top goal scorer with 43 goals, creating a post-war Celtic record. Reason enough to be happy. But that was the least of the achievements for him and the team.

What a difference a manager makes; Celtic came out in August 1965 a different beast entirely, and roared on to eighteen games with just one defeat; against Rangers, 1-2. Celtic under Stein's tutelage were going to be a team playing exciting, forward-thrusting football. The forwards were encouraged to scour the penalty area for free space, and the results were almost frightening. They hammered in goals against Aberdeen, 7-1, Heart of Midlothian, 5-2, Stirling Albion 6-1 and continued to demolish the opposition mercilessly, hitting the first place in the league in January 1966.

They were by then proud possessors of the Scottish League Cup for the first time since 1958, and what's more, they had beaten Rangers in front of over 100,000 people, 2-1, to get it. The old rivals were no longer in charge and Celtic were back on top. They were in two more finals that season, neither of which they could quite turn their way: the Scottish Cup went to Rangers by the narrowest of margins, 1-0, and the European Cup Winners' Cup went to Liverpool in the replay, 1-2 on aggregate. So close. Yet now there was reason to be proud again. Proud fit to burst, because the team had many more gems to show the fans.

They were on top of the league table after a 3-2 win against St. Johnstone and there they stayed, coming in ahead of Rangers by two points at the end of the season; unthinkable just twelve months before. The 5-1 league win in a revenge defeat of Rangers, was a juicy memory as Celtic took the championship they had craved since last winning it in 1954.

Stein had engineered an incredible turn around in the club's fortunes. What extraordinary hope bubbled to the surface at Celtic Park; what a magical time to wear the green and white kit or scarf. Stein's rock-solid belief in his team, his knowledge of the individuals who played in it, and awareness of their strengths and weaknesses had worked miracles on the field; the players' confidence soared. But the new boss had only just started, and he wanted nothing less than everything.

The season of 1966-67 will go down in history. Writers ran out of superlatives to describe the Bhoys early on, and just a glance at the final tables reveal a team that simply rampaged through the opposition, unstoppable in every competition they entered. Celtic fans only had to mourn three losses; two of them to Dundee, oddly. The team were top of the table all season except for one week in March 1967. It was phenomenal. The warning to all came when Celtic dissected Rangers 4-0 in the Glasgow Cup in August 1966. On the 7th of November, the Glasgow Cup became the first trophy, when Celtic beat Partick Thistle 4-0. The steamroller was underway.

In December, Willie Wallace joined the team just before Joe McBride had to leave for an operation. McBride was in extreme pain because of a disintegrating kneecap that kept him out of the team for the remainder of the season. As Billy McNeill intimated, McBride and Wallace might have been the duo of the decade had fate not intervened.

But the team was now not reliant on just one player. As the league wins mounted, so too, did the scything League Cup victories. There was not one slip, right up to the final, as they pounded St. Mirren 8-2, and Dunfermline Athletic 9-4 on aggregate to meet Rangers on the 29th of October 1966. No wrong moves this year. Celtic brought home the honours for the second consecutive year, with a 1-0 victory.

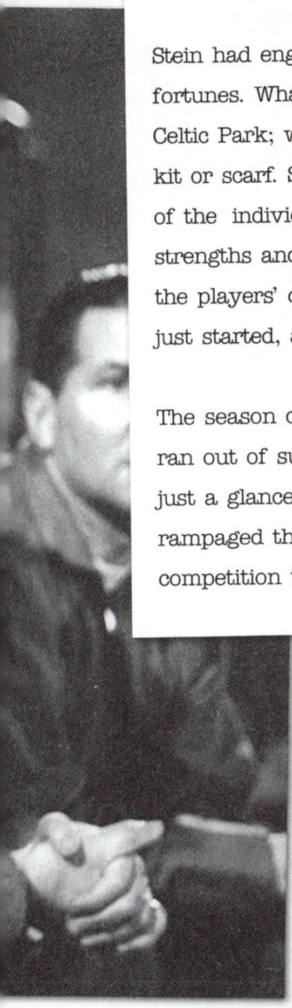

1967 CELTIC TEAM

THE GOLDEN YEARS

And that was just the start.

They powered through the league and fourteen games without defeat from the seventh of January 1967; as though that wasn't enough, they were devouring the opposition in the Scottish Cup, too. Elgin City disappeared under a wave of seven goals, and Queens Park sank 5-3. On the 29th of April 1967, Celtic were at Hamden Park for the Scottish Cup final against Aberdeen. It was not one of the best finals Hampden Park had seen, but two goals from Willie Wallace made sure that Celtic would end the game as winners.

On the 15th of May 1967, Celtic became Scottish League champions, closing the season on 58 points, three ahead of Rangers, whose domination of Scottish football was well and truly over.

Sensational as the season had been, the club had an eye on raking in the biggest success of all; The European Cup.

The club had reached the final in Lisbon against mighty Italian star team, Internazionale; if they could pull off the victory, Jock Stein and his men would go down in Celtic history as legends. As McNeill, Johnston, Wallace, Chalmers and their teammates walked on to the pitch on the 25th of May 1967, they were singing the Celtic song, and Scotland's pride in its own went with them. Big Jock unceremoniously turfed the interloping Inter manager off the Celtic bench and the game began.

Celtic intended to attack the renowned Italian defence from the start, but it was a penalty in the seventh minute that had the Italian fans sensing victory. Undaunted, Celtic continued to take the game to the Italians, who were was saved only by the efforts of their goalkeeper, Sarti. When the Glaswegians returned to the dressing room at half-time the score was still 1-0, and the Scottish team knew that they could crack the Italian defence.

On the 63rd minute they were proven right when Jim Craig's cross found Tommy Gemmell, whose twenty-yard shot beat the Italian keeper to level the scores.

With nervous excitement at fever pitch and the end of full time approaching rapidly, Gemmell passed to Bobby Murdoch with just five minutes left to play. Murdoch's shot headed towards the goal, ricocheted off Chalmers and into the Italian net. The Celtic roar could be heard in Glasgow. The legendary Lisbon Lions had performed the unimaginable; given Celtic five trophies in one season, and become the first Scottish side, indeed the first British side, to have conquered the European Cup; a season of success on a staggering scale. Many of the Lisbon Lions have passed away, but the wonderful games that those and other Celtic legends of the field created, are burned into the hearts of Celtic fans everywhere.

So, how to follow a season of superlatives?

25TH MAY 1967 EUROPEAN CUP FINAL LISBON, PORTUGAL. CAPTAIN BILLY MCNEILL LEADING OUT HIS CELTIC TEAM. CELTIC 2 - INTER MILAN 1

25TH MAY 1967 BILLY MCNEILL CELEBRATES WITH THE EUROPEAN CUP AND POLICE AFTER BEATING INTER MILAN 2-1 AT LISBON, PORTUGAL

Almost impossible, but the Bhoys went for it with the skill and vigour for which they had become renowned in such a short space of time. They proved that this time, Celtic were the team to watch for the foreseeable future. Not so much a case of 'would they win trophies' but 'how many would they win'.

The league season for 1967-68 – the International Board now limited goalkeepers to taking four steps with the ball – was hugely successful as the statistics show; only one match was lost; against Rangers, the second game of the season, 1-0. That was it. Three draws, and a race to the top against a powerful Rangers side, which was decided only by the Ibrox club's last match against Aberdeen. Rangers lost 3-2 at home, and Celtic, with a game in hand, were league champions again.

The Scottish FA Cup and the European Cup were lost in round one of both competitions, which was a severe disappointment so early in the season. The Scottish League Cup was a different story, though, and saw an effervescent squad hammering home the goals; 7-1 in the semi-final against Morton. In the final, Dundee fought bravely, but were eventually washed away with a 5-3 defeat.

So, a season that finished with a double of League and League Cup can hardly be called anything but hugely successful. Especially for Bobby Lennox, who was top goal scorer with 44 goals, a tally that has only been bettered by Jimmy McGrory and Henrick Larsson. The awful events and appalling behaviour of the South American teams during Celtic's failed excursion into the Intercontinental Cup competition that season are best glossed over. Jock Stein's comment says it all; "I would not bring a team to South America again for all the money in the world."

Three league championships in a row for the Celtic Bhoys; the last time that had happened was in 1916. This time around there were three League Cup victories to go with them.

Celtic fans now looked forward with eager anticipation to the start of a season. And with George Connelly joining the club – a man with the potential to become a world-class player attaining the standing of German player Franz Beckenbauer, as one writer has said – who knew what glories might come their way in terms of thrilling games and trophies? So far as that goes, 1968-69 was another season of scintillating football that would highlight Celtic's domination of the Scottish game. Losing 2-4 against Rangers at Ibrox in the second game for the second season in a row was a hard bone to swallow, and at Celtic Park this time. Ouch. Bhoy, that hurt, of course.

But it was irrelevant, in fact, as were the other two defeats that season. Rangers again, 1-0, and Morton at home 4-2. What? Well, we should at least give plucky Morton their due credit.

Also irrelevant because Celtic were top of the table from the sixth game until the end of the season, and were champions for the fourth time with 54 points, five points ahead of Rangers.

The last league game took place on the 30th of April; Celtic had gained the treble by then because they had also lifted the Scottish League Cup, 6-2 against Hibernian; there had been a fireworks display of goals during that competition which included a thumping of Partick Thistle 6-1, and a wicked 10-0 destruction of Hamilton Academical. And then there had been another famous victory in the Scottish Cup.

That one had taken place four days before winning the league; on the 26th of April. Jimmy Johnstone had been suspended, but Gemmell, Auld, Murdoch, Chalmers, Willie Wallace and the other Bhoys ran out for a fiercely-contested Old Firm match. Celtic were not going to let this one away, and Billy McNeill rocked the Ibrox men on their studs with a headed goal after just three minutes.

BILLY MCNEILL AND OSCAR MARTÍN, CELTIC FC AND RACING CAPTAINS (RESPECTIVELY) SHAKING HANDS BEFORE THE INTERCONTINENTAL CUP PLAYOFF HELD IN MONTEVIDEO, URUGUAY

The game was evenly balanced although petty fouls and aggressive incidents took the gloss from the play at times. Celtic began to heap on the pressure, and within two minutes just before half-time, Connelly and Lennox put the game beyond doubt – short of the Celtic team going home after forty-five minutes, that is. Stevie Chalmers' goal was the icing on the cake in the second half, and Celtic won the Cup 4-0. The second time they had won all three honours within three years. An extraordinary achievement.

The game of football is nothing if not unpredictable. Celtic lost four games in the 1969-70 season, one more than the previous season, and had a bit of a struggle to get to the top of the table. It took them until December and a 7-2 demolition of Dundee to do so. They still ended as champions – as fans now expected them to do! – with 57 points, having left Rangers far behind on 45.

What was happening elsewhere?

Well, this was a season of three cup finals, but just one cup, and that was won early on in the final of the Scottish League Cup competition. Celtic started off by belting Airdrieonians 6-1, and winning the final 1-0 against St. Johnstone.

The Scottish FA Cup went to Aberdeen, 3-1 in a match that left Stein shaking his head at the referee's decisions. After one of their best results ever, 3-0 against Benfica of Portugal, and winning on the toss of a coin in the replay, Celtic beat Leeds United 1-0, and then, with Jimmy Johnstone in outstanding form, 2-1 in the semi-final of the European Champions Cup, the famous 'Battle of Britain', only to lose the final against Feyenoord, 2-1. Billy McNeil admitted that the team was guilty of complacency on the day, underestimated the Dutch side, and were lucky to get away with the final score.

Another Scottish double, though, and a terrific start to a new decade. What a difference to ten years before when Celtic had started out into the sixties on ninth place, facing many more seasons when one disappointment would follow another. What a decade for the stalwarts of the team such as Auld, Chalmers and Fallon, who had seen in both decades with Celtic!

The seventies would present new excitement for the fans with the emergence of the 'Quality Street Kids', a group including Danny McGrain, Kenny Dalglish, Davie Hay, Lou Macari and George Connelly.

The 1970-71 league season was slightly more sticky than Celtic had been used to since Jock Stein's arrival at Celtic Park. It was also the season when tragedy darkened Ibrox. 66 fans were killed in a crush towards the end of the match against Celtic on the 2nd of January 1971. All rivalry forgotten, the whole of Glasgow was in mourning.

Aberdeen and St. Johnson served as Celtic's rivals in place of Rangers, who only finished 4th that season. With Harry

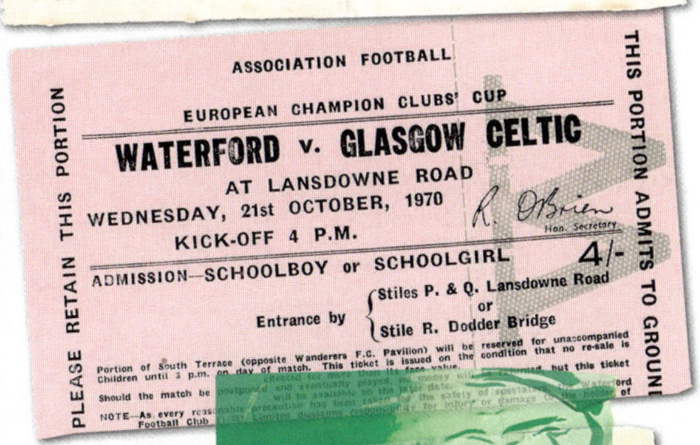

Hood taking over the top goal scoring honours, adding thirty-three to his tally, Celtic proceeded to lash the goals home against any team that wasn't looking properly; 5-0 and 6-1 against Clyde, 5-0 against Motherwell, 8-1 against Dundee, 5-1 against Cowdenbeath. Those results belie the fact that the team provided slightly unsteady performances, which put them on first place for eleven games, then dropped them to second place for seventeen games, before a nail-biting finish put them back on the top spot for the final two games with 56 points; two ahead of Aberdeen.

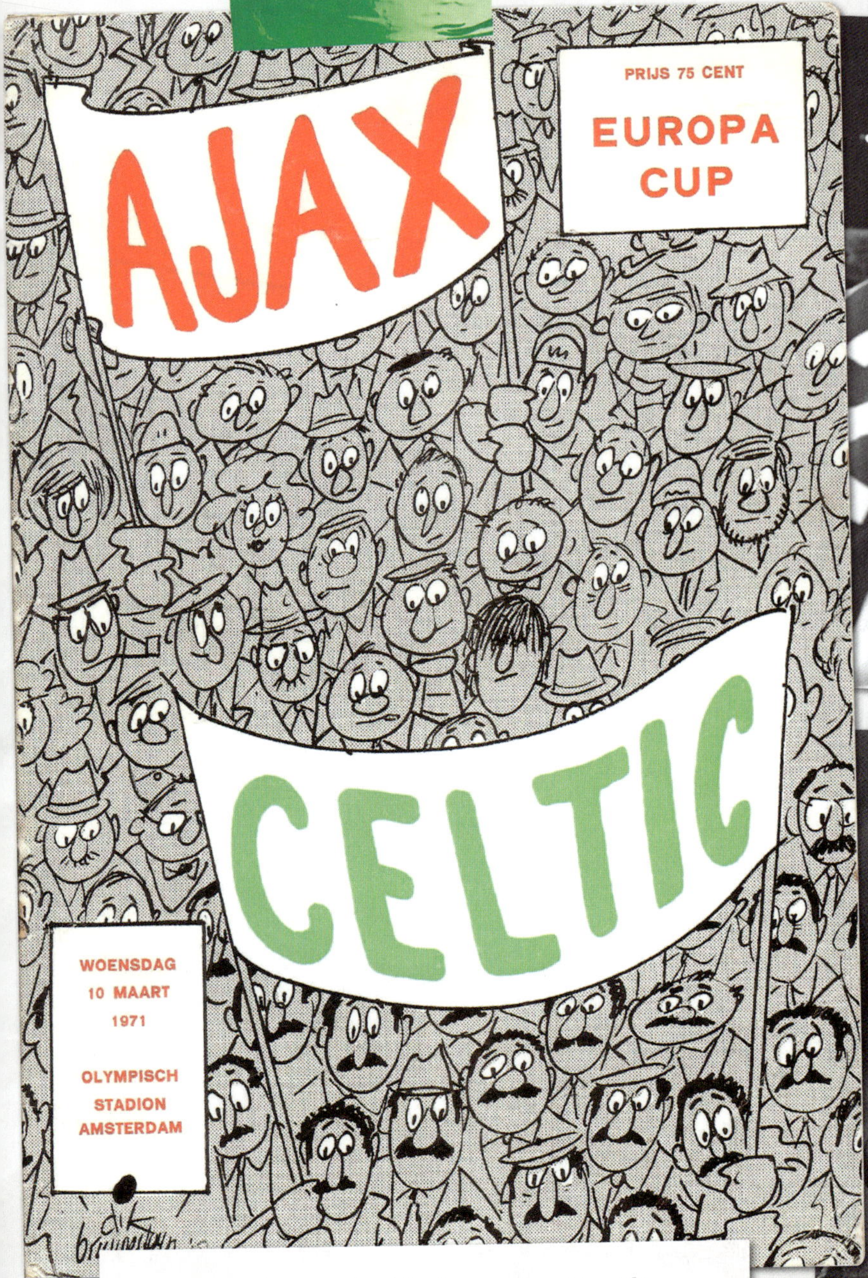

TROUBLE BREAKS OUT IN THE EUROPEAN CUP QUARTER FINALS, AGAINST AJAX, 1971

Celtic made hard work of the League Cup, too, only vanquishing Dundee after four matches, with a 5-1 victory. Unfortunately, they went down 1-0 to Rangers in the final. But there would be a glorious retaliation for that defeat. The European Champions Cup was lost to Ajax in the quarter-finals, so the only cup competition left was the Scottish FA Cup. Celtic made it through to the final, after frightening their fans with a 1-1 home draw against Dunfermline Athletic and a 3-3 draw against Airdrieonians, only to come up against Rangers in the final, which ended in another 1-1 draw. So the fans went on to watch a replay on May 12th with their hearts in their mouths.

They need not have worried. The newspaper headlines afterwards showed that they had been given a match to remember. "A Jimmy Johnstone Spectacular . . .", and, "Johnstone Magic", they trumpeted. In an exciting game in which Celtic played better football with "brilliant style", Macari slid in the first goal after 24 minutes, and when Johnstone was brought down after breaking clear for goal a minute later, the penalty was sent home by Harry Hood. When Rangers' Derek Johnstone came on, the Ibrox men pulled one out of the hat on the 58th minute, but it was not enough. The whistle sounded, and Celtic had beaten Rangers for the first time in a cup final replay.

EUROPEAN CUP QUARTER FINALS, AGAINST AJAX, HANDING OVER OF THE CLUB PENNANTS, 1971

Kenny Dalglish's four-season reign as top goal scorer – interrupted by Deans and Wilson – began with another championship title in 1971-72. That was the season in which Dalglish scored 29 goals in total and began his rise to fame in the top echelons of British football.

In the second game, Rangers were the adversary. Celtic laid down the rules with a 3-2 win at Ibrox, and went on to dominate the table for most of the season. They lost to St. Johnstone at home, 1-0, in the fifth game, and to Heart of Midlothian, 4-2 away in April 1972, in the penultimate game. In between, there had been more scintillating football to delight fans, who could now shout encouragement from a new stand that had been completed in September 1971.

This was a season when Clyde were given a complete hiding, 9-1 in the very first match of the season; when Dundee crumpled under a 5-1, onslaught as did Partick Thistle, Kilmarnock and Motherwell. It was a season when fans were treated to a rare tidbit; Rangers were beaten again in the league, 2-1 at Celtic Park. When the final match of the season was drawn, 1-1, against Dundee, Celtic had 60 points, 10 points clear of Aberdeen, with Rangers again far behind on 44 points. That would remain Celtic's best tally until 1987.

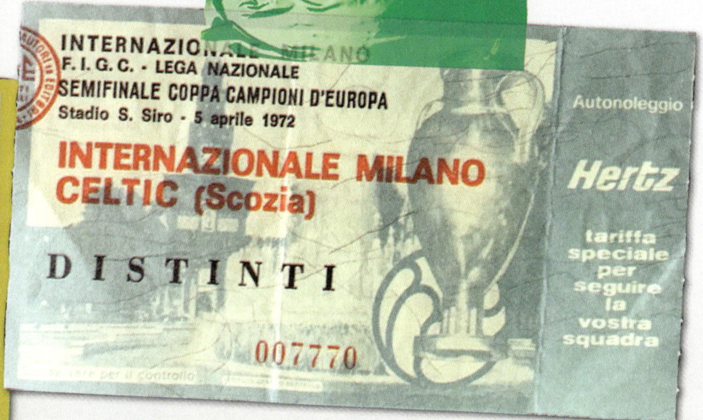

CELTIC'S BOBBY MURDOCH IS SHADOWED BY ALEX MACDONALD OF RANGERS, 1971

It was also a season of three cup finals: the Scottish Drybrough Cup, the Scottish League Cup, and the Scottish FA Cup. And Celtic made the headlines in October 1971, for all the wrong reasons. They lost the final of the Scottish Drybrough Cup in August 1971, to Aberdeen, 2-1. Then they were on the wrong end of one of the biggest post-war upsets in Scottish football in October 1971 when they lost the Scottish League Cup final to Partick Thistle, by the ridiculous margin of 4-1. Partick Thistle were four goals up after just thirty-seven minutes, and it was a huge embarrassment which Stein did not wish to be subjected to for a second time. Before long he had signed John 'Dixie' Deans, (who was serving out a six match ban at the time) and Wallace, Hughes, Chalmers, Clark and Gemmell departed to other clubs.

After that debacle, there was a great run in the European Champions Cup, which was only stopped in the semi-final by Inter Milan, who won on penalties after two drawn games, 0-0.

Fortunately, the league title was retained at the beginning of May 1972, and on the sixth of the month, Celtic were able to celebrate a famous win in the Scottish Cup Final against Hibernian with a 6-1 goal festival. Dixie Deans popped in a trio of goals, the first Celtic player to do so in a Scottish Cup final since Jimmy Quinn in 1904. Deans' second goal has gone down in the history books as one of the best ever seen from a Celtic player. Having intercepted an attempted Hibernian clearance, Deans went around the Hibernian goalkeeper, moved towards the goal along the by-line, outmanoeuvred a defender before rounding the goalkeeper again and firing the ball into the net. The spectacular somersault that Deans then executed has since become a TV favourite. The final score meant four Scottish Cup wins in six years for Celtic; an impressive haul.

Another season of three cup finals followed, but for the first time in seven years, none of the trophies were held aloft by Celtic players. Hibernian emerged the winners against Celtic in both the Drybrough Cup in August 1972, 3-5, and the Scottish League Cup in December 1972, 2-1. The European Champions Cup was lost in November 1972 in the second leg of round two against Ujpest Dozsa, 2-4 on aggregate.

Thankfully the team's form in the league was holding up. Dalglish was superb, and top goal scorer again, hammering in thirty-nine this time - ten more than the previous season. Scotland's sports writers named George Connelly as Footballer of the Year. There was a 3-1 victory against Rangers early on in the season. The big victories continued to build up; 6-2 against Kilmarnock, 5-0 against Motherwell, and 6-1 against Dumbarton. But Rangers were having a good season as well, and so the race to the top of the table became tense as the season progressed. The final fourteen games passed without defeat, but the battle for first place would be decided by the final game of the season against Hibernian, who had already knocked Celtic out of two cup competitions. Fortunately, the scoreline was 3-0 in Celtic's favour and Celtic lifted the league championship for the eighth time. Very fortunately, as it turned out, because when they met Rangers in the final of the Scottish Cup one week later, they lost 2-3. It was a bitter pill to swallow.

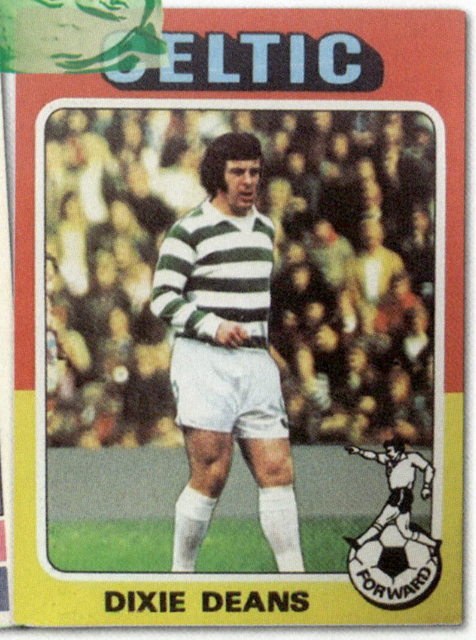

The ups and downs on the field were mirrored off the field, too; Jock Stein had been hospitalised in January 1973 with a suspected heart attack. Lou Macari went south to join Manchester United, and Bertie Auld and John Fallon had also played their last games for Celtic.

Celtic equalled the world record for a succession of league championship wins, when they racked up their ninth consecutive title at the end of the 1973-74 season. They were, perhaps, lucky to do so, because their total of 53 points was the lowest since they had begun their extraordinary award-winning run under the guidance of Jock Stein. They still had the ability to score shovelfuls

GLASGOW RANGERS' DEREK PARLANE CHALLENGES FOR THE BALL WITH JIM BROGAN OF CELTIC, 1973

KENNY DALGLISH COMES OUT TO DO BATTLE, 1974

of goals, putting seven past Partick Thistle, and six past Falkirk, Dunfermline Athletic, and East Fife. But seven games drawn and four lost meant that the points tally was less bountiful than in previous years. But as Hibernian and Rangers did even worse, with 49 and 48 points respectively, Celtic were on top of the table from their eighth game until the end of the season.

Cup success returned, too, in 1974. Once again, the Drybrough Cup and the Scottish League Cup had been lost in the final, 0-1 in both matches, to Hibernian and then Dundee, and the European Champions Cup challenge foundered against a vicious Atlético Madrid team - three Spaniards sent off and seven booked. Celtic lost 0-2, after the second game.

In the Scottish Cup final, however, Celtic put three goals past Dundee United without conceding one themselves. In a match that Celtic never looked like losing, Harry Hood's performance was outstanding, and rewarded with a goal, and the Bhoys emerged victorious to claim the League/ Scottish Cup Double, the fifth time they had done so with Jock Stein at the helm.

At the end of the season, another mighty Celtic stalwart left the team; Davie Hay took his talents to Chelsea. There was trouble, too, with the gifted but erratic George Connelly, whose absences had become an increasing problem for the manager. Connelly was uncomfortable in the limelight, disliked the cut and thrust of modern football, and would make only 23 first-team appearances in the 1974-75 season, and just three thereafter.

Nonetheless, it seemed as though Celtic would lift another league title, as they started out in the autumn of 1974 with a 5-0 win against Kilmarnock. There was just one defeat in nineteen games, and that had been against Rangers, 2-1, at Celtic Park. But then Celtic crashed. There were 8 more defeats to come before the end of the season, both home and away. There was to be no title this season. Celtic were third in the table. Their 45 points were far behind a resurgent Rangers with 56.

But if the league had produced disappointing results, the cup runs would offer compensation. Once again, there were three cup finals to look forward to; the Drybrough Cup, the Scottish League Cup, and the Scottish FA Cup. The Scottish Drybrough Cup went to Celtic in August 1974, when they beat Rangers on penalties after a 2-2 draw. So that was one memory to treasure. The European Champions Cup campaign ended in the second round against Olympiakos, 1-3 on aggregate. In the Scottish League Cup, however, old rivals Hibernian could not stop the wash of Celtic goals as they went down 6-3 to the Glaswegians. In May 1975, Celtic lifted the Scottish FA Cup by beating Airdrieonians 3-1.This was the second time in five years that Celtic had won two Scottish FA Cup finals back to back.

A decade had passed since Jock Stein had taken over at Celtic Park, a decade of unprecedented success for Celtic. No one could have wished for him to have to go through what happened shortly after the end of the 1974-75 season. Stein was driving home to Glasgow from Manchester airport, when he was involved in a head-on collision and was rushed to hospital in Dumfries, where he was operated upon. Stein had almost died in the crash; later, friends would testify to the fact that mentally, he was never quite the same man again.

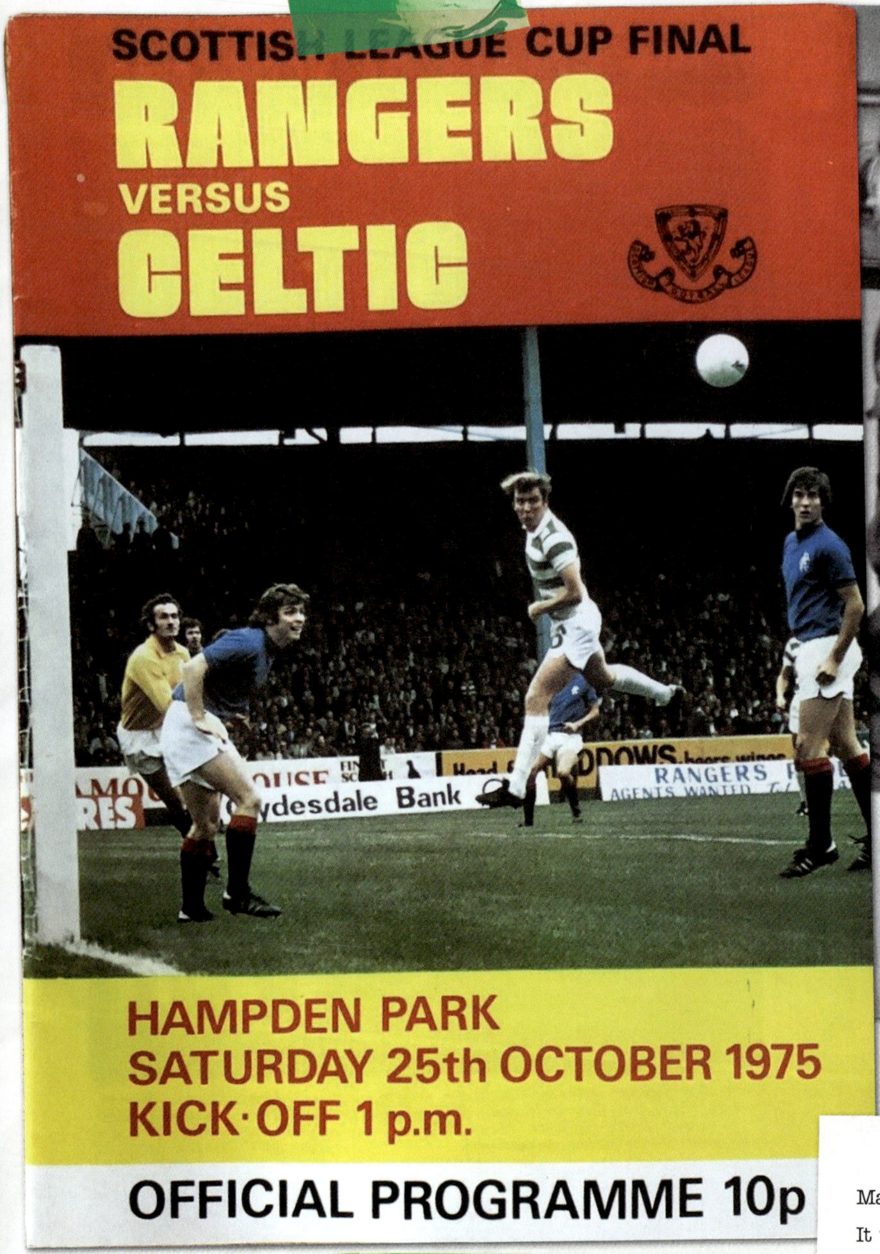

Many people realised that the end of an era had arrived. It was an abrupt ending: the winds of change were blowing through Celtic Park. Jimmy Johnstone and Billy McNeill had taken off the hooped shirts for the last time; Johnstone had moved on, McNeill had retired. The season that followed, 1975-76, was the worst that Celtic had endured since 1965; there were no trophies, there was no league title. It seemed to be a portent of things to come. This was the first season of the newly-formed Scottish Premier Division. There were only ten clubs competing for the title, so teams played home and away twice; Celtic came in second behind Rangers having lost to their Glasgow rivals twice, drawn twice and been defeated by them in the League Cup final, too. Sean Fallon had taken

Confidence seemed to return to the club immediately, and although there were some sticky periods Celtic challenged hard for the title and took it from their Old Firm adversaries decisively, with 55 points, to Rangers' 46.

That was not the only glory that season, for although the League Cup was lost in the final to Aberdeen, 1-2, and the UEFA Cup challenge petered out in the second leg of the first round against Wisla Krakow, 2-4 on aggregate, there was great news from the Scottish Cup final.

Celtic had lined up against Rangers once more. True, it was a lacklustre game, but the important thing was that the penalty goal by Andy Lynch secured a Celtic victory and another League/Cup double for Jock Stein.

THE 1975 GLASGOW CUP FINAL CONTESTED BETWEEN RANGERS AND CELTIC AT HAMPDEN PARK ON THE 10TH OF MAY, 1975

over as manager until former Partick Thistle man David McParland was given the job for the latter part of the season. Stein was not happy with the choice, about which he had not been consulted. He knew that McParland would be considered automatically for the managership should Stein leave the post free, and was of the opinion that a Celtic man should have been chosen. Nonetheless, the results from the 1976-77 season prove that the two men got along well at work. There were new faces on the field, intended to prevent a recurrence of the previous season; Pat Stanton in midfield, Joe Craig and Alfie Conn. But there was no Harry Hood, no Dixie Deans and no George Connelly.

By now, Kenny Dalglish and Danny McGrain were the last of the "Quality Street Kids", and their number was reduced still further in August 1977 when Dalglish signed for Liverpool after 320 appearances with Celtic. Celtic fans were not happy with his decision. On top of that, Pat Stanton and Danny McGrain were both victims of injury. Luckily, some very promising players were starting to make an impact; midfielder Tommy Burns, for example or Roy Aitken in defence and George McCluskey up front.

The 1977-78 season was a very difficult one for Celtic. A glance at the results table for the season shows that they did not win a single one of their first five games and lost five games in a row from the end of December. It was clear that something was very wrong. The season was littered with lost games and they were fortunate to come in on fifth position at the end of the season; but they were almost 20 points behind the leaders Rangers. They struggled in the Scottish FA Cup and the European Champions Cup before they were eliminated, and lost in the final of the Scottish League Cup, 1-2 to Rangers. It was painfully clear that without the old Jock Stein, nothing would be quite the same again. By the end of the season, Jock Stein's career at Celtic was over, and one of the most glorious periods in the club's history had come to an end. Stein's tally of successes had been truly astonishing by any scale of measurement. He had helped

1978 RANGERS V CELTIC
JOHN DOYLE ON THE BALL

the club to ten league titles, seven Scottish Cups, seven League Cups and a European Champions' League Cup.

In May, Celtic approached Billy McNeill, former captain of the "Lisbon Lions", to offer him the position of manager at the club. He accepted.

McNeill was popular with the fans. But did he possess the skill and man-management abilities for which Jock Stein was known?

Had the golden years come to an end?

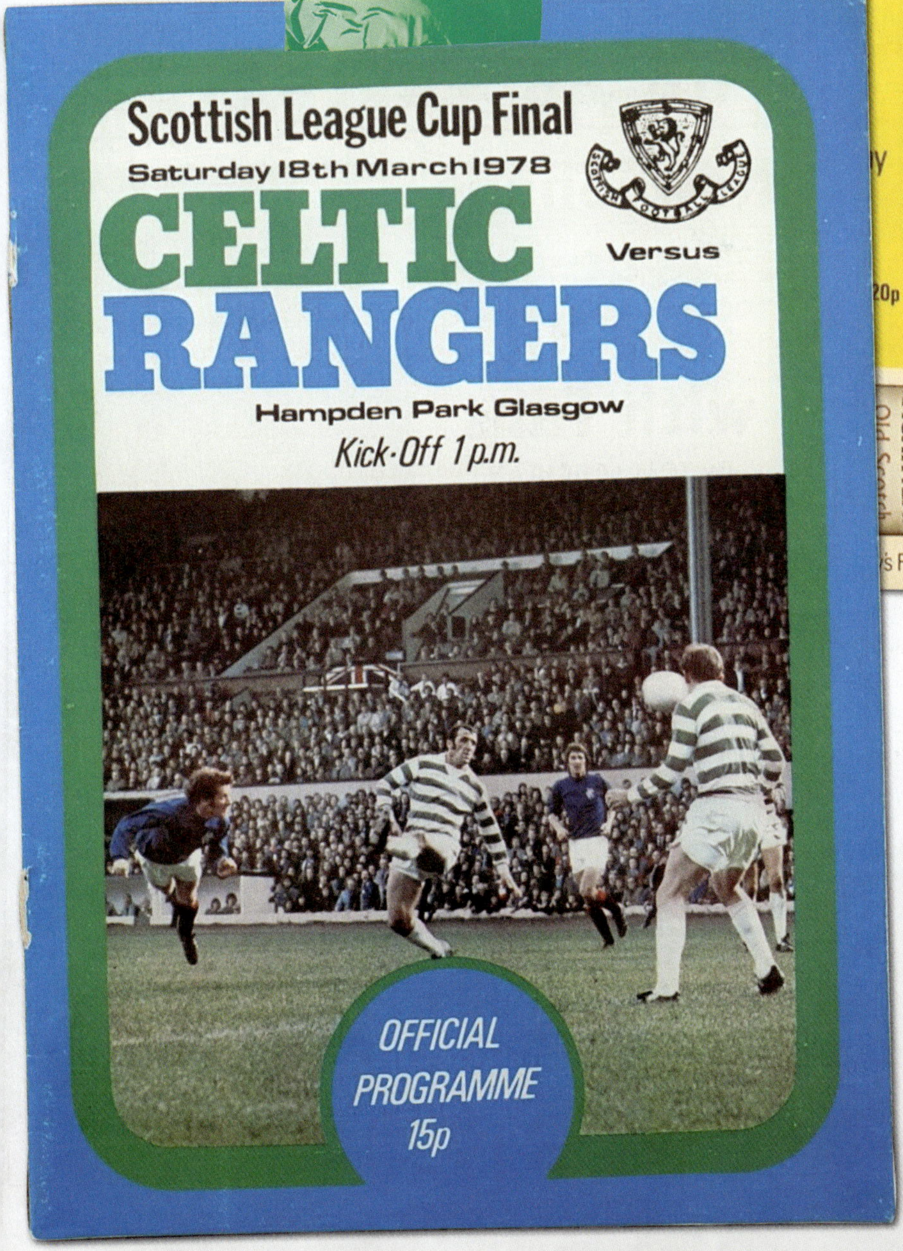

DOUBLE TROUBLE

When "Caesar" McNeill took over, he told the board of directors that they needed to spend money if they wanted to continue to achieve success. The result was that winger Davie Provan and midfielder Murdo MacLeod arrived at Celtic Park, two astute acquisitions.

To everyone's relief, the season got off to a good start in autumn 1978 and Rangers went down 3-1 in the fourth game. From then on, Celtic's form deserted them; they were in eighth place after a 1-0 victory against Aberdeen in March 1979, having come through a terrible period when they won just one game out of eleven. The league title seemed unlikely, and Scottish Cup dreams vanished in the match against Aberdeen in round five when they lost 1-2 at home the same month. The League Cup challenge had already been stopped by Rangers in December, and in the Anglo-Scottish Cup, Celtic had been silenced by Burnley, 1-3 on aggregate. It seemed that Celtic fans would be looking back longingly to the past from a present that was worryingly uncertain at best.

They lost 1-0 to Rangers in May, after which no one was left with any expectations. But the bhoys fought on, and when they met in an Old Firm match, the last game of the season, and sent Rangers home with their tails between their legs after a 4-2 victory, Celtic had snatched the league title. It was an extraordinary game, with Celtic 1-0 down at halftime and 3-2 in the lead with one minute left to play. When McLeod slammed home the fourth, the crowd erupted with joy. It was a glorious moment for the new manager McNeill and his men. It had been a close run thing, however, and McNeil knew that he needed new blood.

BILLY MCNEILL

Rangers' challenge sagged in the season of 1979-80, and despite an indifferent season themselves, with seven losses and eleven draws in the league, Celtic were on top of the table for most of the time. But their poor showing in the second half of the season allowed Aberdeen to slide to the top by one point. All of the other competitions had ended in disappointment, except the Scottish FA Cup which took place a week after the end of the league season.

Against Rangers.

Once more, Celtic took the honours by a hair's breadth, 1-0. Sadly, an invasion of the pitch by Rangers' supporters with violence on their mind marred the occasion and resulted in both clubs being fined £20,000 by the SFA.

ANDY LYNCH

ROY AITKEN

Not one of Celtic's better seasons; George McCluskey's 17 goals as top goal scorer proved that; but neither had it been one of the worst. Yet it was fairly obvious that from now on, Celtic supporters would have to be content with one, and if they were lucky, two honours each season.

In 1980-81, the honour would be the league title, McNeill's second as Celtic manager. Worryingly, tensions were running high between the chairman Desmond White and the manager. McNeill could be forceful, and his priorities were to field the best team he could, whilst the chairman was worried about falling gate receipts and kept a tight reign on the finances.

The season produced 56 points for Celtic, which was enough to take the title, three ahead of Aberdeen in second place. The team had been made to fight hard, though - fortunately new keeper, Irishman Pat Bonner proved to be a rock of stability between the posts - and there were only two 'goal feasts'; 7-0 against St. Mirren, and 6-0 against Heart of Midlothian. Fun to watch, anyway...

There were no cup finals. Elimination at the hands of Dundee United was Celtic's fate in the semi-finals of the Scottish FA and League Cups. They fell in round one of both the Drybrough Cup and the European Cup Winners' Cup competitions. A bitter experience for a club used to constant success for so long. Winning the league may have been the pinnacle of achievement for other clubs, but McNeill knew that more was expected of him, and the pressure showed in his behaviour, resulting in disciplinary problems. Desmond

1979 RANGERS GOALKEEPER PETER MCCLOY TAKES THE BALL FROM CELTIC'S JOHNNIE DOYLE

White felt that McNeill's behaviour was unacceptable. Not exactly a good way for a club to start out on a challenge for top honours.

The wonderful game of football can wrong-foot the casual observer in the blink of an eye. So it was that Celtic now created a record by hugging the number one spot in the league for the entire season and taking home their thirty-third League Championship. Only Rangers and Dundee United had managed to get three goals past Bonner, once each.

The Scottish League Cup, the Scottish FA Cup and the European Champions Cup were disasters, pure and simple.

A Celtic legend, Paul McStay had made his first team debut in January 1982; his skill would soon earn him the nickname, 'The Maestro'. Both McGarvey and Nicholas had suffered broken legs.

Snakes and ladders with a vengeance.

Charlie Nicholas, later described as the "most exciting player to emerge in Britain since George Best", had made his debut for Celtic in 1980 aged 18. In 1982-83, he made his presence felt in the first team as a player of first-class ability, with a superb season that made him top goal scorer with 48 goals and brought him talks with the top clubs in Britain.

CELTIC . . . 3

RANGERS . . . 2

LAST-GASP CELTIC

"Only" one honour at the end of this season again, and this time it would be the Scottish League Cup, which Celtic had last won in 1974. A particularly rewarding victory this for captain Danny McGrain and his squad, because the opponents were Rangers. Davie Provan dribbled, passed and crossed like a man inspired and helped Charlie Nicholas and Murdo MacLeod to the two terrific goals that won the trophy. Nicholas scored a beauty, left-footing the ball into the net whist surrounded by Rangers players, and MacLeod smacked in a drive from 18 yards.

Rangers pulled one back, but couldn't get past Celtic again, and the day's triumph belonged to the Bhoys.

In the league, Celtic came to rue their defeat by lowly Motherwell, because Dundee United took the title by just one point from them in an exciting season that had produced several big wins for the Glasgow side; 7-0 against Motherwell, 5-0 against St. Mirren, 5-1 against Morton, 5-0 against Kilmarnock; and three more defeats handed out to Rangers; 3-2, 2-1, and 4-2 at the end of the season, sending supporters into the summer with happy memories.

TBALL CLUB · RANGERS FOOTBALL CLUB
BROOMLOAN ROAD STAND
FOLLOW YOUR TICKET COLOUR
ENTER BY TURNSTILES 57-60 and 71-74
BLUE SECTION REAR
ROW 9 SEAT No. 19
SCOTTISH PREMIER LEAGUE
RANGERS v. CELTIC
IBROX STADIUM
SATURDAY 1st NOVEMBER, 1980
KICK-OFF 3.00 p.m.
£3.00
RANGERS FOOTBALL CLUB LIMITED
In the event of the game to which this ticket refers being postponed or re-arranged for any reason, the ticket will be valid for the altered date or kick-off time. On no account will money be refunded.
THIS PORTION TO BE RETAINED BY THE HOLDER
RANGERS FOOTBALL CLUB · RANGERS FOOTBALL CLUB

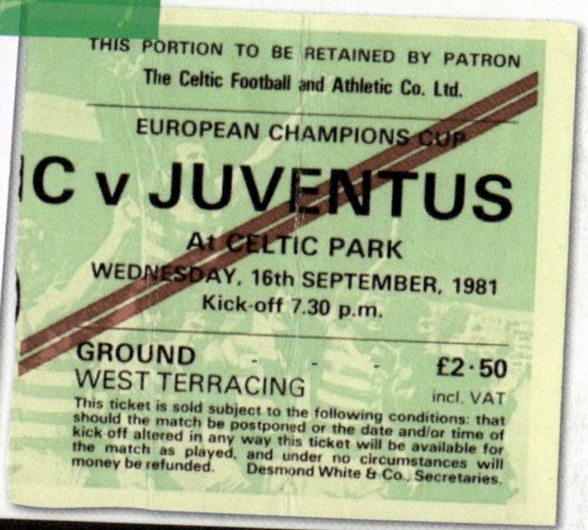
THIS PORTION TO BE RETAINED BY PATRON
The Celtic Football and Athletic Co. Ltd.
EUROPEAN CHAMPIONS CUP
IC v JUVENTUS
At CELTIC PARK
WEDNESDAY, 16th SEPTEMBER, 1981
Kick-off 7.30 p.m.
GROUND - - - £2·50
WEST TERRACING incl. VAT
This ticket is sold subject to the following conditions: that should the match be postponed or the date and/or time of kick-off altered in any way this ticket will be available for the match as played, and under no circumstances will money be refunded. Desmond White & Co., Secretaries.

THE GLASGOW CELTIC FOOTBALL TEAM, AT PARKHEAD IN GLASGOW, AUGUST 1981.

Those memories were worth a great deal because the summer was one of turmoil at Celtic Park.

With the end of the season came the end of Charlie Nicholas's brief career at Celtic. The buying power of the big English clubs was simply too great, and in June he signed for Arsenal. McNeill was devastated. Nicholas's potential was never fully realised afterwards; perhaps, with hindsight, he should have stayed and been nurtured for a little longer. That might have helped both his and his manager's careers. But it was not to be.

McNeill's own career at Celtic ended shortly after Nicholas departed. Manchester City had expressed an interest in acquiring McNeill's services, and after a newspaper story about his dissatisfaction with certain aspects of his treatment at Celtic, the club's relationship with its manager bounced onto the floor, and his days at Celtic Park were over. For the time being.

So, for the time being, were the glory days. Celtic FC had come to a crossroad.

One of McNeill's protégé's, Brian McClair, had been signed without fuss in May 1983. He proved to be the lightning rod in the Celtic attack in the intensely frustrating season of 1983-84, and was top goal scorer for four consecutive seasons.

George McCluskey departed for Leeds United in July, assistant John Clark was let go with a golden handshake, reserve coach Frank Connor became assistant manager, and then David Hay came through the revolving door to become Celtic manager.

Hay brought in new players: Brian Whittaker from Partick Thistle, John Colquhoun form Stirling Albion, for example. The results were mixed. Celtic's challenges in every competition came to nothing, and fans were left to contemplate the fall from grace that Jock Stein's accident had precipitated.

First things first.

The UEFA Cup continued without Celtic when they lost to Nottingham Forest 2-1 on aggregate in December 1983. The run had included a massive 5-0 thumping of Sporting Lisbon, though. If only…

Then, they had made heavy work of it, but arrived in the Scottish League Cup final against Rangers, whose own form had been less than sparkling. Celtic lost 2-3, struck down in extra time having come back from 2-0 down. It was a bad moment when a good one was badly needed.

In the league, they had been unable to produce the edge that would topple Aberdeen, and seven losses were enough to strand them on second place, seven points adrift, with 50 points. So when they met Aberdeen in the Scottish Cup final on the 19th of May 1984, no one would have bet that Celtic would come out on top.

They didn't.

It was close, though, to give them their due, against a high-flying Aberdeen side. Celtic took them to extra time, and had lost Roy Aitken, who was sent off, so they had fought valiantly. Nonetheless, the 2-1 scoreline was in Aberdeen's favour.

Rather surprisingly, White did not remove David Hay after that season of ill-fortune.

SFA CUP FINAL – CELTIC V RANGERS – GEORGE MCCLUSKEY IS HUGGED BY FRANK MCGARVEY AFTER SCORING THE WINNING GOAL FOR CELTIC, 10 MAY 1980

MORE SNAKES

While might have wished that he had got rid of David Hay as August 1984 turned into September, because by then Celtic had only won one of their first five games and drawn all the others, and already been dumped out of the Scottish League Cup quarter-final by Dundee United, 2-1. Before the middle of December, the European Cup Winners' Cup was also no longer of any concern to Celtic, thanks to Rapid Vienna and a clash that merited that description. Tommy Burns was punched by a Rapid Vienna player, which led to injuries, assaults by spectators, suspensions, fines for both clubs; it was all there in a litany of the worst aspects of the game. At any rate, Celtic eventually lost the tie and that was that. One to forget.

League form improved sufficiently to maintain second place; Aberdeen were not to be displaced, and took the title for a second year running, seven points clear of Celtic again.

JIM MELROSE OF CELTIC GOES PAST RANGERS DAVE MCPHERSON DURING AN OLD FIRM MATCH AT PARK HEAD, SEPTEMBER 1983

21ST APRIL 1984 CELTIC V ABERDEEN, DANNY MCGRAIN IN CONTROL

1984 ROY AITKEN OF CELTIC IS BOOKED BY REFEREE A FERGUSON

One last hope remained.

The Scottish Cup final.

Celtic's only final that season drew them against Dundee United, who had beaten them twice in the league. It would be a tough call.

Celtic supporters needed nerves of twisted titanium to last through to the end of that 100th Scottish Cup final.

The first half was tepid and produced no goals for either side. Dundee seemed to have clinched it with a goal after 54 minutes. It was hard to see what Celtic could pull out of the bag, until Hay reshuffled the team, putting Aitken in midfield and bringing on McClair.

AITKEN'S FINEST HOUR!

AUGUST 1983 GLASGOW CUP FINAL AGAINST RANGERS. RANGERS' IAN REDFORD IS CHALLENGED BY CELTIC'S ROY AITKEN

THAN LADDERS

THE CENTURY

Celtic hit back from the dead

Paul McStay, McGarvey, Johnston, McClair and O'Leary all collected their first Scottish Cup winners' medals. There was guarded optimism in the air.

It seemed odd, then, for Hay to sell McGarvey. It certainly didn't help, in a season that could only just be persuaded to yield some glitter, 1985-86.

Celtic struggled for the first two thirds of the league season, suffering four defeats in five games starting with a loss to Heart of Midlothian in October 1985. They almost came to rue that loss bitterly. They only lost one game in the new year of 1986, but frustratingly drew six almost back to back, and hovered on fourth place before they found their form again in March 1986, and began to crawl back up the table. Three games before the end of the season they were on second place, having beaten both Dundee and Motherwell by a 2-0 margin, and were in a knife-edge

And suddenly, Celtic began to fire on all cylinders. In what was described as a "pulsating" last quarter of an hour, Provan sent home a spectacular bending free kick inside the Dundee left-hand post, on 76 minutes; Celtic were even and hell bent on victory. When Aitken whipped his cross over to McGarvey, a flying header put Celtic in the lead. Dundee couldn't recover and the Bhoys had won their first trophy for manager David Hay, to begin a five-year period of success. Celtic had come back, if not from the dead, then from having one foot in the grave. Bonner, Willie McStay, McAdam,

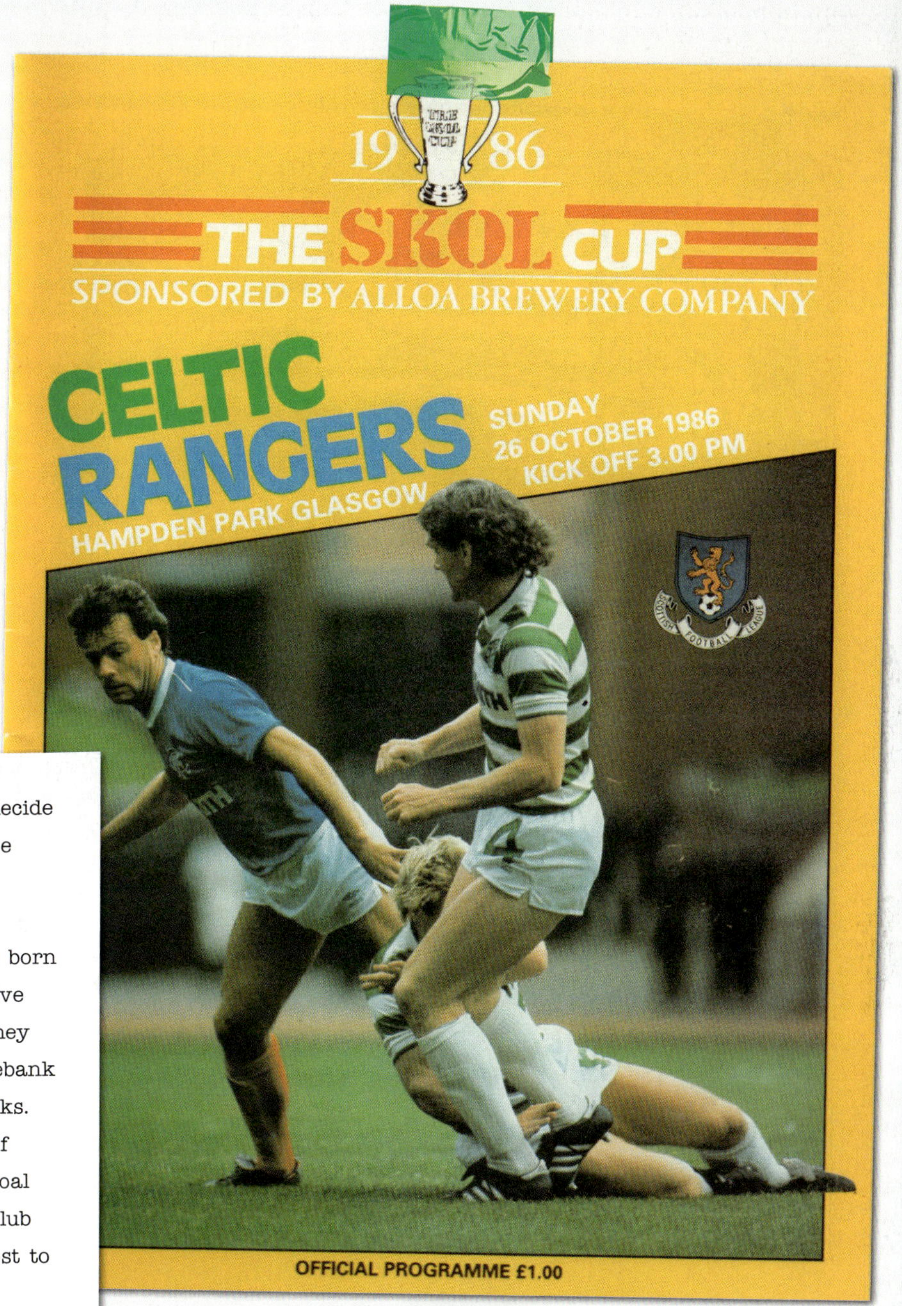

race with Hearts for the title. The last match would decide it all; Celtic needed to win by a large margin and hope that Hearts would lose at third-placed Dundee.

And the gods of football decreed that Celtic should be born aloft that year, and ordered them to hammer home five against St. Mirren away from home. The third time they had won by five goals that year; Hibernian and Clydebank had also been on the receiving end of the Celtic attacks. It was a good time to repeat the feat. Oh yes, what of Hearts? They lost 2-0, so Celtic were champions on goal difference. The year had been a damp squib for the club in the other competitions, so this win was a vital boost to a team struggling to come to terms with mortality.

The team's vulnerability settled in to create havoc in the 1986-87 season, even though they got off to a sparkling start; unfortunate, because 1987 was the club's centenary year. Rangers were now spending heavily and they had

TERRY BUTCHER HITS THE DECK AFTER A CHALLENGE FROM CELTIC CAPTAIN ROY AITKEN, 1986 SKOL CUP FINAL

the edge throughout a season in which Celtic could only beat their rivals once in the five encounters they had. The most difficult defeat of all to deal with was the one that Celtic suffered in the Scottish League Cup final in October 1986. Celtic had made heavy work of the competition, scraping through both the quarter and semi-finals on penalties.

But Rangers took the league trophy 2-1, after a controversial penalty decision.

But the league challenge was going well and they were on a run that would see just one defeat - Rangers, 1-0 - in twenty-one games, and several large scorelines for comfort; at one stage, their lead at the top was ten points.

Six losses and two drawn games in the new year left them six points behind Rangers at the end of the season. The European Champions' Cup and the Scottish Cup competitions were distant memories by then. For the second time in four years Celtic had finished without any honours. The only aspect that was remembered with satisfaction was Brian McClair's personal best of 41 goals in his fourth season as top goal scorer.

Change was inevitable now.

Danny McGrain had played his last game for the club as had Alan McInally, Murdo MacLeod, Maurice Johnston, and worst of all, Brian McClair; so too had Davie Provan who retired due to ill health.

Neither would David Hay survive the summer. He was sacked, having refused to resign, and his replacement was announced the same day; it was Billy McNeill, returning to Celtic for the third time.

McNeill had mighty problems to solve, and although the new manager's presence brought about a sense of relief and hope in improvement, no one was under any illusions as to the scale of the problem the club faced. Was McNeill going to be the man to turn the ship around?

Billy Stark from Aberdeen, Chris Morris from Sheffield Wednesday and Andy Walker from Motherwell were brought in to try and make sure that he was. Roy Aitken was given the captaincy.

Nervous excitement greeted the start of the new season in September 1987. Celtic were out of the blocks like lightning, and after the third consecutive victory, against Motherwell 4-1, McNeill's stock was running high, especially after Celtic reached the quarter-finals of the Scottish League Cup. Beating Rangers in the league, 1-0, helped, too.

But the good work had already begun to unravel as August progressed, and indifferent form lasted through to October. When it returned in October, they had been pushed from the Scottish League Cup and the UEFA Cup by Aberdeen and Dortmund, respectively, and a match against Rangers which had resulted in the criminal prosecution of four players, was also behind them. The game ended 2-2, one of the least happy of the Old Firm clashes.

Celtic were now on second place.

So, two awards down the tube, two to fight for.

League form returned, so that Celtic swiftly took over the top place at the end of November 1987, and were still there when the Scottish Cup matches began in January. Hope dared to flare again in the fans' hearts. The miracle they so fervently wished for began to take shape, and then arrived in a blaze of glory. Two new faces at Celtic Park, Frank McAvennie from West Ham and Joe Miller of Aberdeen had been brought in to help make it happen.

Just one game was lost in the new year, against Heart of Midlothian. It mattered not because with McAvennie, Stark and Walker thumping in the goals, 18, 13, and 32 apiece, Celtic had opened up an unbeatable lead in the league, and they put paid to Hearts in the quarter-final of the Scottish Cup, setting up a meeting with Dundee United in the final. What had been unthinkable was now almost tangible. The Double.

One disquieting fact on the 14th May 1988 was that keeper Pat Bonner was on the sidelines, suffering from a back injury that had required surgery.
The first half of the final showed that the game could go either way, so Celtic fans were being sorely tested; neither side had the advantage, and the score was 0-0 at half-time.

Forty-nine minutes into the second half, Celtic nightmares came true when Kevin Gallacher put Dundee ahead. It was all or nothing now and Celtic turned up the heat. But Dundee held firm. Stark and McGhee came on for Whyte and Walker with twenty minutes remaining ... and Celtic found renewed vigour. In the 76th minute McAvennie was there to head in a Thomson cross to set the score level. The game entered the ninetieth minute and another Celtic attack took shape. McAvennie found the ball at his feet and an opening in the defence, and when his close-range shot got through and beat the Dundee keeper, Celtic had come back from being a team in decline the previous season to being Scottish Cup and League double winners. What a way to end the club's centenary season.

What would they do the following season?

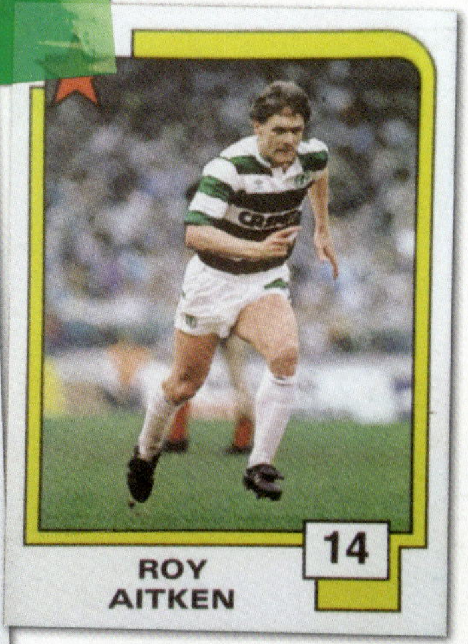

14TH MAY 1988 SCOTTISH FA CUP FINAL, CELTIC 2, DUNDEE UNITED 1, THE BHOYS CELEBRATE

Zip fairly niftily down the ladder again was the answer. Yet that 1988-89 season was only a herald for worse to come, so let's get stuck in to the last really good news for a while.

You would have to go back to autumn 1977 to find a worse start to a league season; eight games, five defeats. Including the ghastly 5-1 plunder carried out by Rangers. Celtic eventually clawed their way from ninth to third place at the end of the season, challenged hard by Dundee United and Aberdeen. They were ten points behind the league champions, Rangers. Something was rotten in the state of Celtic Park.

The League Cup and the European Champions' Cup had slipped away, too. The only hope to be coveted was in the Scottish Cup where Celtic had sped through to the final with what used to be their customary ease. To meet Rangers.

Was it overconfidence by the league champions that prevented them from repeating the trick from earlier? The lack of Ray Wilkins? It was a somewhat lacklustre match by all accounts, and Ranger's manager Graeme Souness came on to try and liven things up a bit. Nothing helped. Joe Miller pounced on a weak back pass to the Rangers' keeper Woods in the forty-first minute, and Celtic had snatched the Treble from Rangers' grasp. It was Celtic's twenty-ninth Scottish Cup. A time to celebrate indeed.

Then the curtain came down.

1989 ROY AITKEN HOLDS UP THE TROPHY AS THE TEAM CELEBRATES WITH THE SCOTTISH CUP

THE FAMINE

McAvennie had gone, McGhee had gone. Polish striker Dariusz Dziekanowski arrived. Paul Elliot arrived. If anyone had suspected that a five-year period without a trophy had begun, there may have been drastic changes during that summer of 1989. As it was, McNeill kept his job and one of the most dismal league seasons in Celtic history lurched forwards on its crutches to the end. Celtic won just one match in the final fourteen; an extraordinary and saddening time. They made it through to the semi-final of the League Cup, only to lose to Aberdeen 1-0. The European Cup Winners' Cup was over in round one. Partizan Belgrade won on away goals after a 6-6 final score. Celtic met Aberdeen again in the Scottish Cup final having beaten Rangers earlier in the competition. Aberdeen won on penalties.

Disappointing losses in an unsatisfactory season.

1990 JOHN COLLINS IS PULLED DOWN BY TERRY HURLOCK OF RANGERS DURING THE SKOL CUP FINAL AT HAMPDEN PARK

1990 FRANK MCAVENNIE GOES FLYING OVER DUNFERMLINE GOALKEEPER DAVE MCKELLAR

Billy McNeill was not sacked. The club's finances were being severely stretched, however, so it was difficult to see what the manager could do to rectify the situation. Billy Stark and Roy Aitken sought their luck elsewhere, and who could blame them. At least they didn't have to endure two lost games to start the new season in autumn 1990, one of which was a 3-0 defeat at home to Aberdeen. Or the loss to Rangers in the final of the Scottish League Cup in October 1990, 1-2. Celtic soon lost touch with the league leaders, slipping to sixth spot in January 1991. The damage couldn't be repaired.

DARIUSZ WDOWCZYK IN ACTION FOR CELTIC, 1990

YEARS

Celtic's improved form from February 1991 did nothing to help, and Rangers were 16 points ahead at the end of the season; Celtic had climbed back to third place. There was no Scottish Cup final this year, either, because Motherwell had put them out in the semi-final, 2-4.

The new chief executive, Terry Cassidy and chairman Kelly were ready for sacrifice. Inevitably, McNeill was the victim. Liam Brady was the beneficiary of the empty manager's seat.

For the next few years, the club was condemned to roll through heavy seas that brought it to the edge of bankruptcy. Bleak times indeed for the proud Glaswegians.

Two managers came and went fairly rapidly as Celtic watched other clubs pass them and take the honours. Liam Brady had no experience of running a team. Players were bought, but the results on the field remained stubbornly mediocre.

1991-92 came and went without loosening the big boys' grip on power; Rangers and Heart of Midlothian took first and second places in the league. Celtic were third, an occurrence that was becoming depressingly familiar, although they were just one point below Heart of Midlothian. The best moment was probably beating Rangers 2-0 at Ibrox for the first time in four years. The worst? Undoubtedly losing 5-1 to Neuchatel Xamax in round two of the UEFA Cup. And losing 1-0 to Rangers in the semi-final of the Scottish Cup. It was like Groundhog Day. Celtic almost there but not quite, never managing to find the cutting edge needed for success.

In his next season at Celtic, Liam Brady was unable to break the Gordian Knot that kept the club doomed to miss out on the trophies. He brought in Rudi Vata, the first Albanian to play in British football, Andy Payton and Stuart Slater. To no avail. League form remained inconsistent, and they achieved third place for the third year running, the fourth time in five years. They drew with ninth-placed Motherwell at home 1-1, twice, and struggled to vanquish relegation candidates Falkirk in three of the four games, and were knocked out by them in the fourth round of the Scottish Cup, 0-2. Aberdeen kicked them out of the Scottish League Cup 1-0, and, again, they could only beat Rangers once in the league, 2-1 at home. Fans desperate for success must have wondered what was going on.

There was a lot going on in fact, off the field. Celtic was the prize in battles to wrest control of the club from an unpopular board, and one man would swim to the top of the pile of groups engaged in the warfare, 'the Rebels', as they came to be known; Scottish Canadian businessman Fergus McCann. The furore would continue into the following year of unrest off and on the pitch.

NEW CELTIC MANAGER LOU MACARI

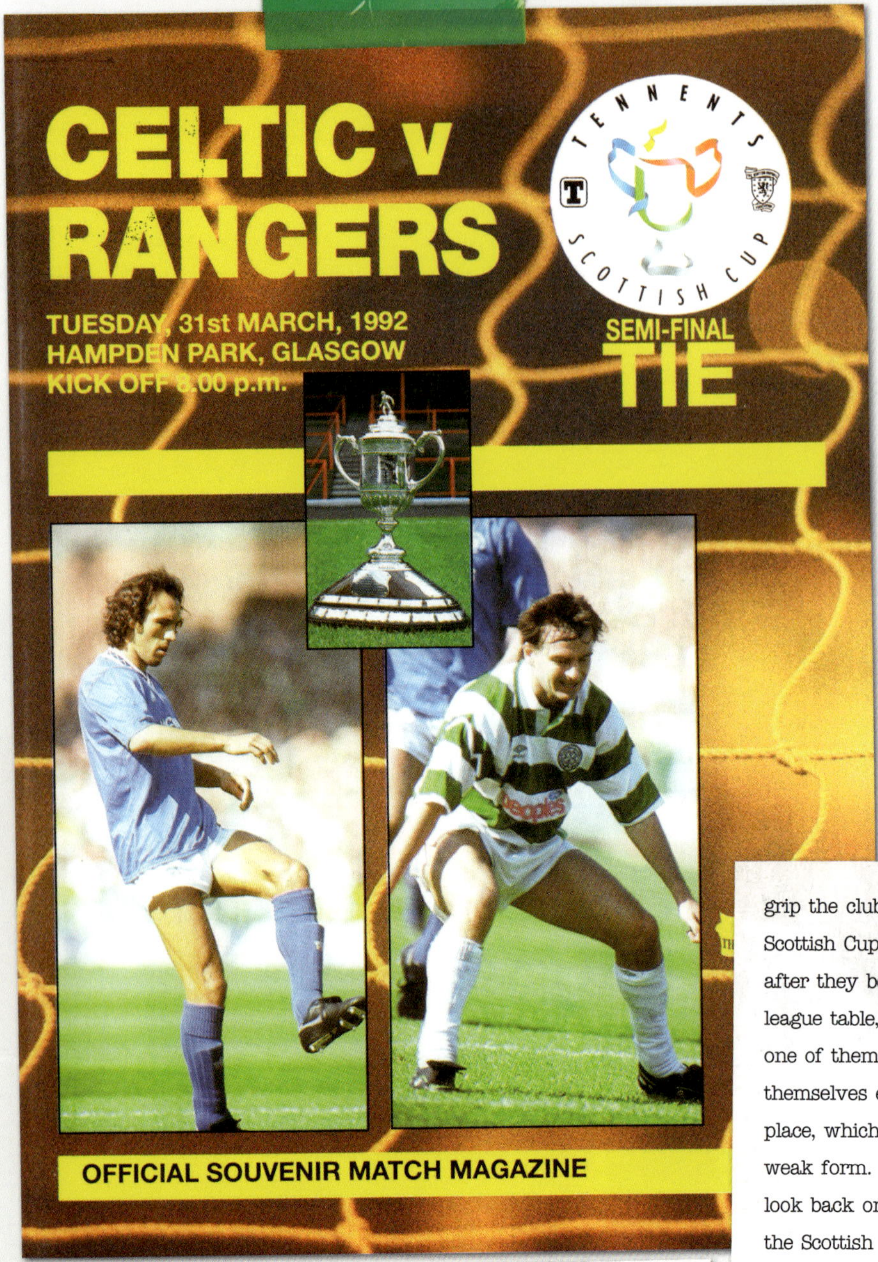

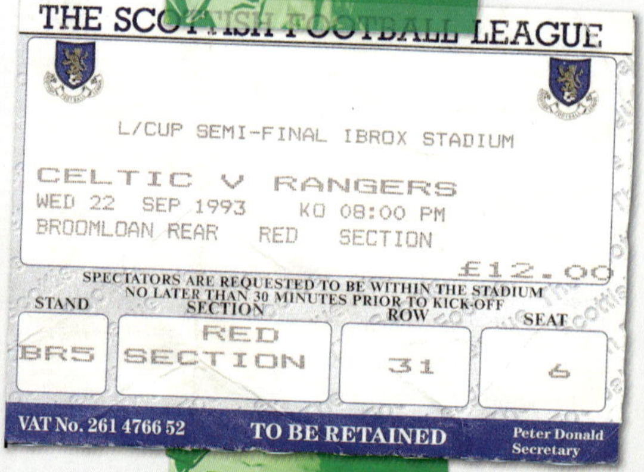

Brady was still in charge as the 1993-94 season got under way. It was to be his last, however. Two victories in the first ten league games, and defeat against Rangers in the semi-final of the Scottish League Cup, 1-0, sealed his fate; he offered his resignation after the tenth game, the third defeat of the young season, against St Johnstone, 2-1, on October the 6th, which left Celtic on ninth place. Brady was replaced with Frank Connor, former goalkeeper, then one of the backroom staff, until Lou Macari took over on the 27th October 1993.

Macari had chosen a bad time, and with everyone's nerves on edge he was to be an early victim of the changes about to grip the club. He could do nothing to stop the UEFA Cup and Scottish Cup challenges disappearing down the plughole shortly after they began. And whilst the club dragged itself back up the league table, victories were proving to be elusive beasts, and only one of them popped up in the final eight matches. Celtic found themselves eight points behind Rangers, the champions, on fourth place, which was something of a marvel in itself considering their weak form. No five goal feasts that season; all that fans had to look back on was a 9-1 hammering of Abroath in round three of the Scottish League Cup. Meager pickings indeed.

Excitement was to found in the boardroom battles as the season ended, and what they would mean for the club.

As early as March, the Bank of Scotland had told the club that as a result of debts exceeding £5 million, the club would be put into receivership. Bankruptcy stood outside Celtic's door.

Miserable days indeed for everyone who loved football in Glasgow.

1994 CELTIC V ARSENAL,
MIDFIELDER, JOHN COLLINS IN ACTION

AN ERA

The fire brigade was on its way, however. Fergus McCann finally ousted the old board of directors, and he and a new raft of directors took over on March the 4th 1994, with just minutes remaining before bankruptcy was declared. In fact, the club was almost £7 million in debt, and with attendances of 20,000 and less, drastic measures were required to keep the club in existence, let alone make it thrive.

McCann formed the Celtic Football and Athletic Company to issue shares that brought in £14 million for the club, a huge success. Celtic had lived to tell the tale.

It seemed that Macari would be next for the knife after such a mediocre season, and with a new man in charge searching for answers. So it proved to be. Macari was dismissed on June 4th 1994. Three familiar faces were brought back to turn the tide; David Hay as chief scout, Tommy Burns as manager and Billy Stark as his assistant. They would take charge during a season in which Celtic would play at Hampden Park while their own ground was renovated.

The new trio presided over a season of two finals, a minor success and a greater success. The league was a pockmarked affair that yielded another fourth place, although Rangers had been subdued twice, 2-0 and 3-0; the first success. They had drawn 18 games, the second greatest number after the 1993-94 season when they had drawn 20, a less happy Celtic record. The Scottish League Cup was only lost on penalties, to Raith Rovers after a 2-2 draw. But for the parched fans came something to shout about at last after five empty seasons.

Celtic reached the Scottish FA Cup final against Airdrieonians.

And won!

1ST OCTOBER 1994 TOMMY BURNS AND ALEX MCLEISH OF MOTHERWELL HAVE A CHAT BEFORE THE MATCH

JOHN COLLINS OF CELTIC CELEBRATES A GOAL DURING A MATCH AGAINST RANGERS AT THE IBROX STADIUM, 27 AUG 1994

That final won't go down as one of the greats, but for a battered Celtic team and its fans, it was water to a man banished in the desert. Paul McStay had taken the captaincy, and the game was basically over after nine minutes when Pierre van Hooijdonk, who had arrived at the club not long before, scored Celtic's goal. But it couldn't have mattered less, and the relief was tangible; it was winning that counted. Celtic had tasted success once more.

Even if it was just for a day and there was a mighty long road still to travel.

However, there were signs of improvement over the following two seasons, even if they did nothing to fill the trophy cabinet.

OF UNCERTAINTY

PETER GRANT CLASHES WITH RANGERS STRIKER ALLY MCCOIST AS PAUL GASCOIGNE (LEFT) AND CHARLIE MILLER LOOK ON. 19 SEPTEMBER, 1995

With just three weeks left in the 1996-97 season, Tommy Burns was sacked. Van Hooijdonk, Cadete and Di Canio also left the club after disputes with McCann, who dubbed them "The Three Amigos", players that Celtic could ill afford to lose. Paolo Di Canio had only joined the club in 1996, and was voted Player of the Year by the Scottish Footballers' Association

Dutch coach Wim Jansen was to be the new team supremo, but he was now to be called head coach, not manager. Assistant coach was Murdo McLeod.

Those two seasons produced almost identical results; second place in the league, an exit in the semi-final of the Scottish Cup and an exit in the quarter-final of the Scottish League Cup. Celtic also bowed out of the European competitions in round two in both seasons. One difference was that Celtic were second in the league table in the 1996-97 season for 34 of the 36 games; and they lost to Rangers four times.

So, with those comparisons out of the way what else was happening? Quite a lot, and the multiplicity of changes began before the season had even ended.

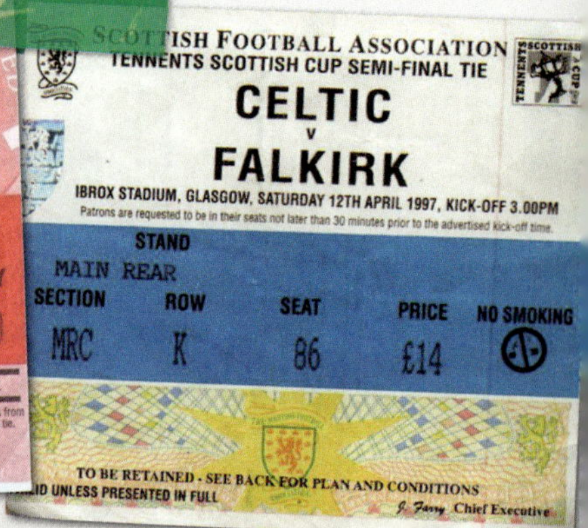

Jansen went on a buying spree. He signed Darren Jackson and Craig Burley, and then Dutch winger Regi Blinker, Stéphane Mahé from Rennes, and Marc Rieper the Danish centre-half. And he brought in a future Celtic hero; the Swedish attacker Henrik Larsson from Feyenoord for £650,000. Jonathan Gould, reserve goalkeeper at Bradford City was another newcomer to Celtic Park in that hectic summer of 1997, which also saw club captain Paul McStay retire due to injury. In his fifteen-year career, he had made 678 appearances for the club.

SCOTTISH FOOTBALL ASSOCIATION
TENNENTS SCOTTISH CUP
SEMI-FINAL TIE
CELTIC
v.
RANGERS
THE NATIONAL STADIUM
HAMPDEN PARK, GLASGOW
Sunday, 7th April, 1996 Kick-off 4.00pm
Patrons are requested to be in their seat not later than 30 minutes prior to the advertised kick-off time.

	SECTION	ENTER BY TURNSTILES	PASSAGE	ROW	SEAT	PRICE
EAST STAND	F	F1-6	29-30	CC	107	£13

TO BE RETAINED - SEE BACK FOR PLAN AND CONDITIONS
IS INVALID UNLESS PRESENTED IN FULL
J. Farry, Chief Executive

UEFA CUP 1ST RND 2ND LEG. SV HAMBURG V CELTIC. PAOLO DI CANIO BATTLES FOR THE BALL AS CELTIC TEAM-MATE PETER GRANT LOOKS ON.... SEPTEMBER 1996

Rangers had now reached nine consecutive league titles, equalling Jock Stein's record, so the search was on for a team that could stop the record passing to Rangers in 1997-98.

What an extraordinary season it would prove to be for Celtic, hinting at the glory days of old, a season that fans would savour.

A season that could not have got off to a worse start in the league; two defeats away and at home, 2-1, against Hibs and Dunfermline. Fortunately, there had been a 7-0 walloping of Berwick Rangers in between, in the Scottish League Cup, or there might have been tantrums at Celtic Park. As it was, the engine then revved up to produce eight league wins. Once Celtic recovered from a stalled engine in November, two more defeats, the club took off again, and by the end of the month they were in the Scottish League Cup final against Dundee United. The new Bhoys, Larsson, Rieper and Burley, all proved their worth with a goal apiece to help Celtic take the trophy for the first time since 1983, with a 3-0 victory. The team had shown that it was capable of taking the silverware again, and optimism returned.

CELTIC CELEBRATE AFTER BEATING ST JOHNSTONE AT CELTIC PARK, TO BECOME THE LEAGUE CHAMPIONS, 9 MAY 1998

In the new year came confirmation that the Celtic men were the equals of anyone in the league, when they met Rangers again. Celtic were four points behind in the league, but they strengthened their own challenge for the title with a 2-0 win that put them on second place. Now the heat was on Rangers. In February, Larsson – in the first of his seasons as top goal scorer with 19 – Rieper, recent new signing Lambert, and the others, dealt out a 5-1 defeat to Dunfermline, and took over the top spot. Rangers were having the fight of their lives against a scintillating Celtic side that would only lose two more matches that season. Both losses made Celtic fans grit their teeth, because both were against Rangers. Both losses had serious consequences.

On the 5th of April, Rangers won the semi-final of the Scottish Cup, beating Celtic 1-2. On the 12th of April Celtic went down 2-0 to Rangers in the league, and fell back to second place. Were the Bhoys going to stumble at the finish and allow Rangers to clinch the title?

Celtic struck back with a 4-1 defeat of Motherwell to claim the top spot again. Rangers then stumbled, losing their penultimate game at Kilmarnock. Which meant that everything depended on the last game. The title was Celtic's to lose. They were up against St. Johnstone at Celtic Park.

No need to describe the atmosphere when Larsson put the first one in after just two minutes! Or when Harald Brattbakk, the new Norwegian striker slotted home the late second goal. Not only had Celtic pulled off a Double, they had denied the Huns their tenth title. Triple celebrations! Celtic could easily celebrate the word ten; they had last won the championship ten years previously.

It seemed that there was to be no pride and joy at Celtic during those turbulent years, however, without tears and anger hovering in the background. Jansen and McCann were not getting along at all, and Jansen was planning his departure even before the celebrations began. It was a blow for the victorious team. Whatever the rights and wrongs of the situation, it seemed that Celtic/McCann had made a big misstep in allowing the situation to lead to Jansen's departure. Dr. Jozef Venglos was appointed to replace him. Dr. Who?, quipped the naysayers. Well, he brought in Slovakian player Ľubomír "Lubo" Moravčík. But he allowed Rangers to take the league title again in 1998-99. The league, by the way, had undergone yet another metamorphosis, and in 1998-99 it emerged as the Scottish Premier League.

Celtic were unable to make headway anywhere. Airdrieonians kicked them out of the League Cup in the first game, 1-0 on August the 19th 1998. On the 26th, the UEFA Champions League challenge was over. Croatia Zagreb, 1-3 on aggregate. In November the UEFA Cup was over thanks to FC Zurich, 3-5 on aggregate.

What about the league? Not good, either, only nine games were won out of twenty in 1998.

Two more defeats in 1999, one of which was handed out by Rangers, 3-0 at Celtic Park, sealed their fate. Second, with 71 points. Rangers had 77. The 5-1 hammering of the Huns in November 1998 had been wasted.

Empty handed, the team entered the summer break to face more disruption. The hapless Venglos resigned although his legacy stood the club in good stead; Ľubomír Moravčík had been joined by Vidar Riseth, the Swede Johan Mjällby and Mark Viduka. Venglos stayed on at the club as European Techinical Advisor.

Kenny Dalglish popped up again as general manager, and John Barnes took over the head coach position. They resided over a mess of a season that had another headline almost before it got underway; McCann announced that his stake in the club was up for sale. The controversial chairman had seen the club become a successful business and the team resurgent,

ENRICO ANNONI OF CELTIC TAKES ON BRIAN LAUDRUP OF RANGERS DURING THE SCOTTISH FA PREMIER LEAGUE MATCH AT CELTIC PARK, 2 JAN 1998

and made a large profit from the sale. Alan McDonald became chief executive and managing director, and Dermot Desmond, the Irish billionaire, was majority stakeholder.

Thank the gods of Celtic Park that the League Cup run ended with a final against Aberdeen which saw the Bhoys emerge as 2-0 winners, because the rest of the season saw Rangers romp home to the league title again with 90 points – having beaten Celtic three times – the

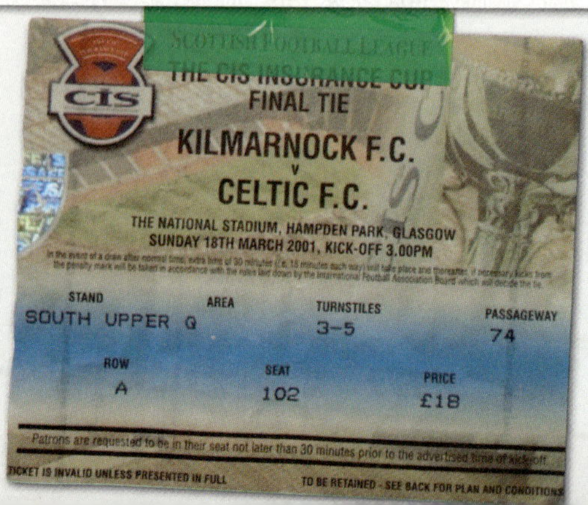

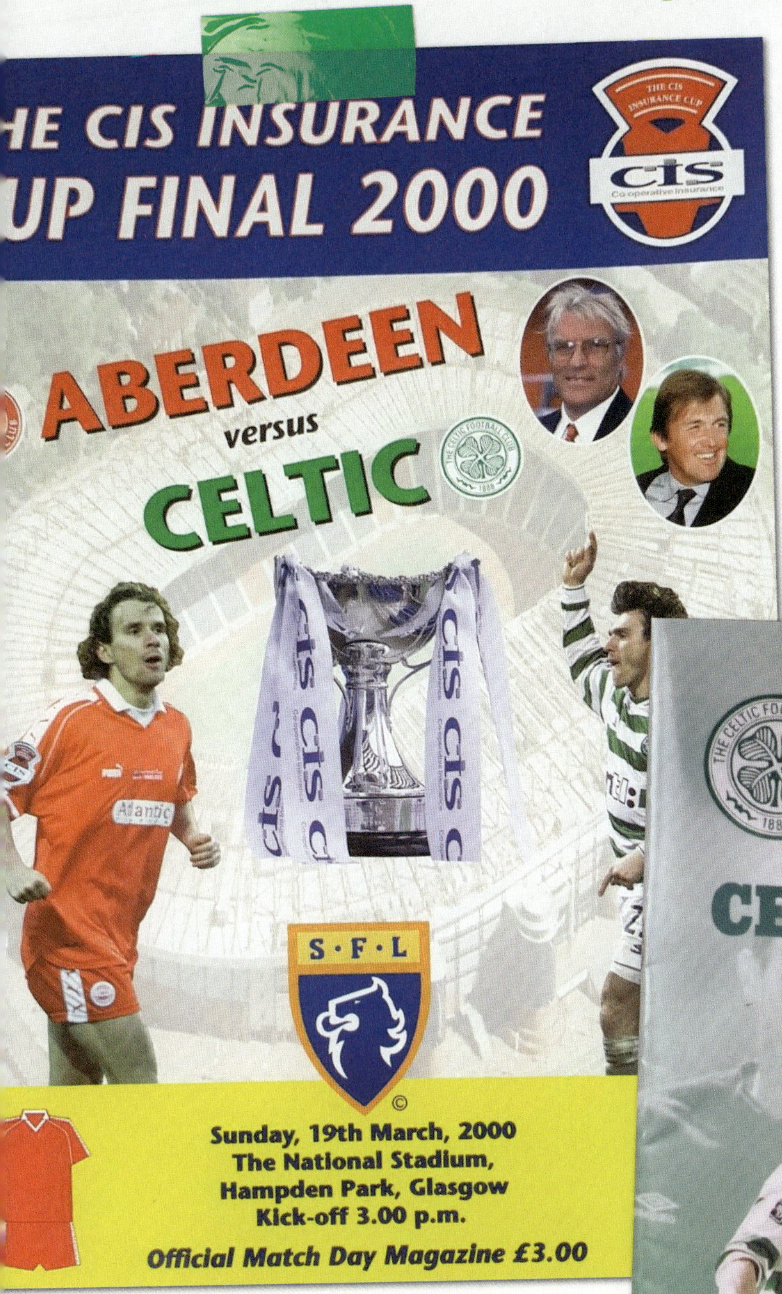

UEFA Cup vanish in the second round, and the Scottish FA Cup vanish in the third round. Not only that, Larsson sustained such a bad injury that it seemed his career might be over. Fortunately not, as we know.

Barnes resigned before the season ended. Dalglish had taken over, and then been sacked at the end of the season. A mess indeed.

A depressing start to the new millennium.

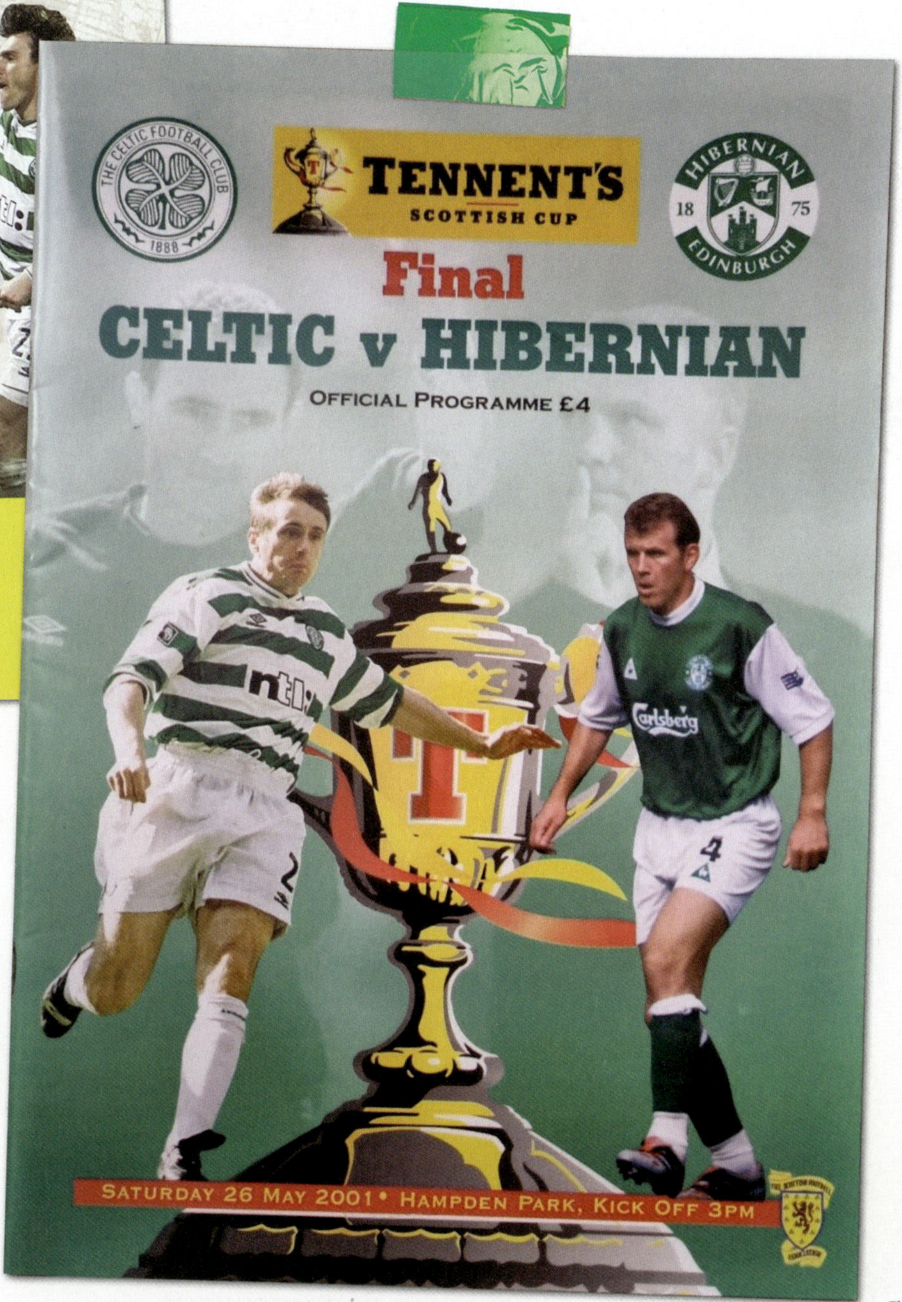

CELTIC'S BRAVE

Oh, brave new world that has such people in it.” What happened at Celtic Park next was worthy of a Shakespeare drama. Are you sitting comfortably?

It's the season 2000-01. A Celtic team starts out in the Scottish Premier League with Martin O'Neill as their new manager – O'Neill brought in Chris Sutton and Joos Valgaeren, soon to be joined by Didier Agathe and Neil Lennon – and after sixteen games without defeat, fans are wondering if they are in the wrong stadium.

Not really. But you get the idea.

Forget the UEFA Cup. Celtic did.

September the 9th 2000, found Celtic at the top of the league table having walloped the stuffing out of Rangers, 6-2 the week before. (Celtic would strike six goals three more times that season; against Kilmarnock, 6-0, Hearts, 6-1 and Aberdeen, 6-0.)

So November came as a bit of a shock. Bordeaux waved the team goodbye in the UEFA Cup on the 9th, and when Celtic met Rangers on the 26th, they collapsed 5-1. Inexplicable … and fortunately a one-off.

Celtic returned to winning form. In March 2001 they took the Scottish League Cup from Kilmarnock in the final, 3-0, having beaten Rangers in the semi-final 3-1. Rangers were beaten again, 1-0, as Celtic headed towards the Scottish FA Cup final and built up a huge lead in the league. Rangers fell again to the unstoppable Bhoys, 3-0 at Ibrox in April as they powered to the league championship with 97 points, their highest total up to that time, and Rangers out of sight on 82.

They had the Double in their pockets, now they were going for the Treble. And with Larsson scoring twice and McNamara once, they lifted the Scottish FA Cup,

7TH APRIL 2001 MARTIN O'NEILL CELEBRATES WINNING THE LEAGUE TITLE

NEW WORLD

18TH MARCH 2001 CELTIC CELEBRATE VICTORY AFTER THE SCOTTISH CIS INSURANCE CUP FINAL AGAINST KILMARNOCK

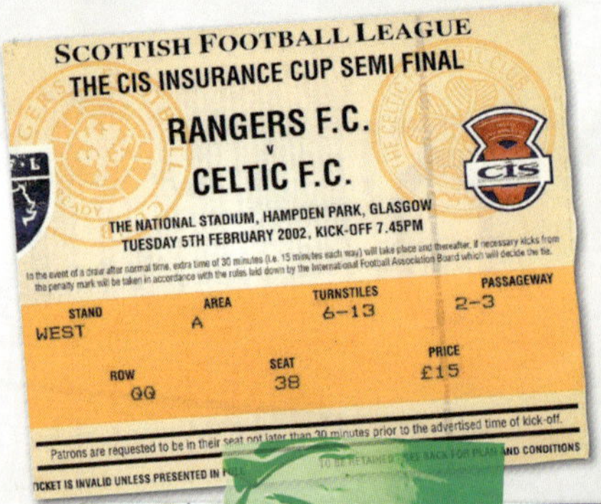

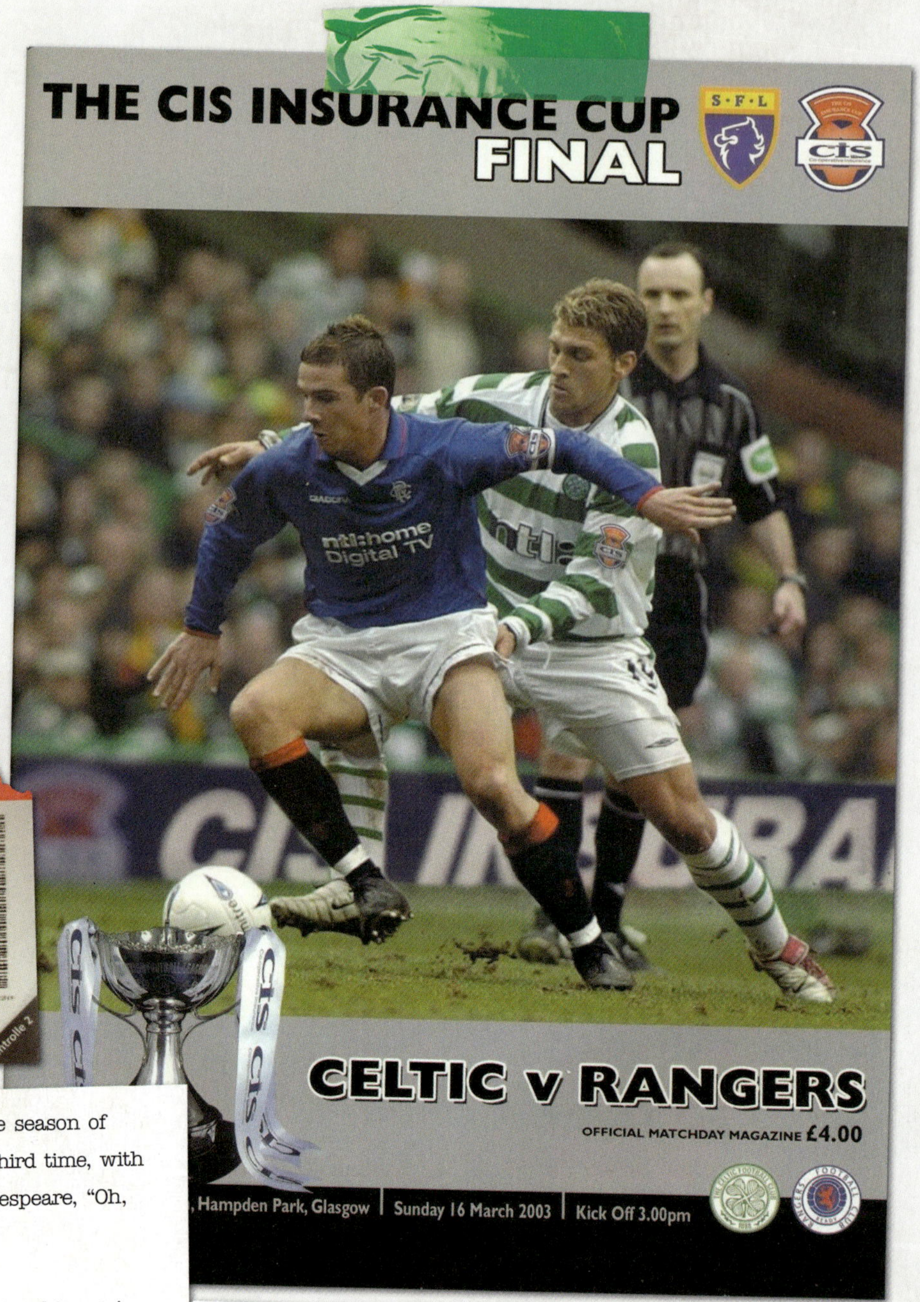

too, 3-0 against Hibernian, to end an incredible season of success. Larsson was top goal scorer for the third time, with a personal best of 53 goals. To rephrase Shakespeare, "Oh, glorious game that has such players in it!"

Martin O'Neill brought home the league championship again the following season as Celtic lost just one game, 0-2 to Aberdeen, drew four, twice against Rangers, and powered to an incredible record-breaking 103 points. They had conceded just sixteen goals, and scored three or more on seventeen occasions. No one could match them; Rangers were trailing second on 85 points when the season ended.

Celtic didn't have it their way in the cup competitions though, and Rangers put them out of the Scottish League Cup, 2-1 in the semi-final and won the final of the Scottish FA Cup 2-3, showing the dominance of the Glasgow sides that season.

All of this meant that the ghastly series of losses in the 2002-03 season came as a horrible and incomprehensible surprise. A manager and team used to brilliant success came back down to earth in the league; three losses and the same number of points as Rangers, 97, lost them the championship on goal difference. They had paid dearly for the match squandered in a 2-1 defeat by Motherwell, who finished bottom of the table. Rangers had the best of it in the League Cup, too, beating Celtic 2-1 in the final. The FA Cup was over in the fifth round, lost 1-0 to Inverness, and when Celtic got to the final of the UEFA Cup at last, having overcome Liverpool and VFB Stuttgart along the way, they lost 2-3 to Porto, whose time wasting and feigned injuries were mean spirited to say the least. Larsson had had a magnificent

24TH NOVEMBER 2004 JOHN HARTSON CELEBRATES THE 1ST CELTIC GOAL DURING THE UEFA CHAMPIONS LEAGUE GROUP F MATCH AGAINST BARCELONA

season again; 44 goals as top goal scorer, and man of the match in the UEFA Cup final. But all the glory of the previous season had vanished; there were more than a few tremors in the Celtic boardroom.

That season proved to be just a blip, however, because Celtic were back fighting for the honours again in the autumn of 2003. Europe proved as hard a nut to crack as ever and yielded no trophies. At home, though it was a different story. The League Cup wouldn't be on the shelf, as Celtic lost 1-2 to Hibernian in the quarter-final. But an impressive thirty-two-game run without defeat, which included

TENNENT'S SCOTTISH CUP FINAL STILIYAN PETROV (RIGHT) TAKES THE ACCLAIM FROM HENRIK LARSSON AFTER SEALING CUP SUCCESS WITH CELTIC'S THIRD GOAL, 22 MAY 2004

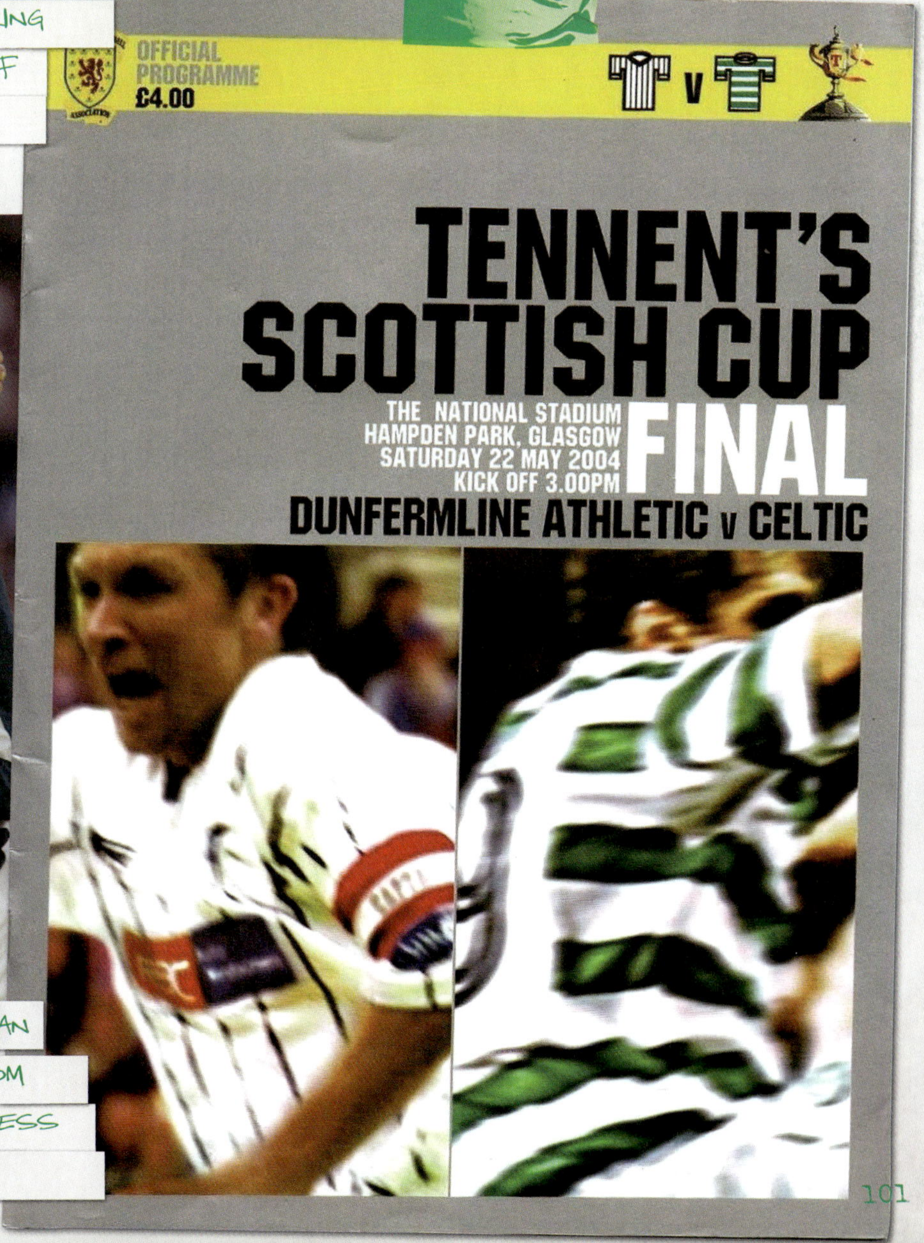

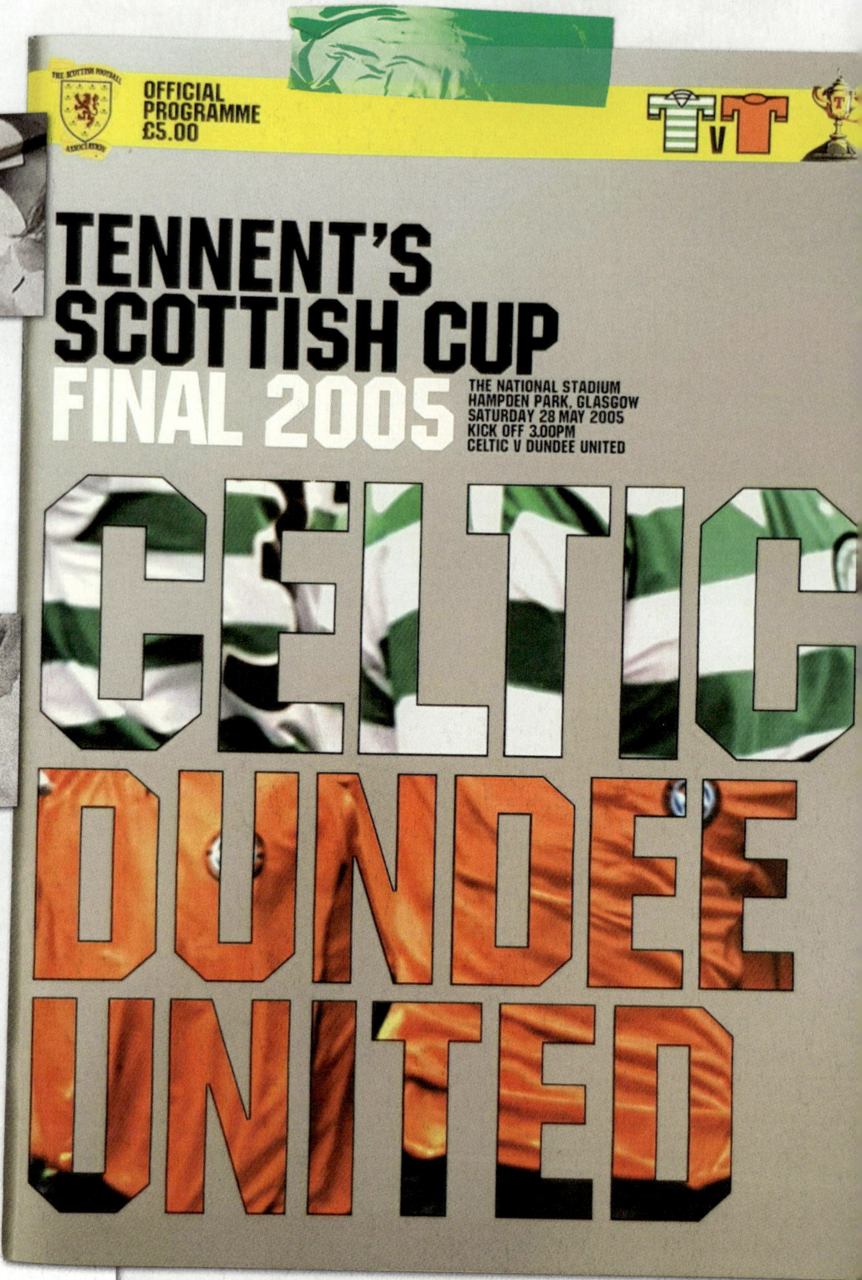

twenty-five consecutive victories, a British record, and twenty-nine victories in all, made them the team to beat in the Premier League as they lashed their opponents with a series of five-goal victories; against Hearts, Kilmarnock and Dunfermline they achieved this total without conceding a goal. Against Hibs it was six, as Larsson went on a forty-one goal spree. Sutton hit twenty-eight and John Hartson eleven in a season in which Rangers fell to the mighty hooped giants four times in the league and once in the Scottish Cup run, the first whitewash of the Old Firm rival in thirty years. And that run ended in the final against Dunfermline and a 3-1 win for Celtic. Which meant that they had the Double again, because they had won the league with 98 points, seeing off Rangers who were once more

left trailing in Celtic's wake with 81. Good times indeed! They were powered by perhaps the best Celtic team ever seen at Celtic Park until then. Martin O'Neill had certainly shown that he was no flash in the pan.

It was with great regret, but with unforgettable memories that fans bade farewell to Henrik Larsson at the end of that season. With 317 appearances and 227 goals, he had a won a place in the hearts of Celtic fans forever with his skill and devotion to the club. He moved on to Barcelona.

O'Neill settled down to his fifth season. It was to be his last at the club, and although he couldn't bring the league championship home – Celtic came second behind Rangers to whom they also lost in the quarter-final of the Scottish League Cup – there was another trophy to send him on his way in triumph. Rangers failed against Celtic as the Bhoys made their way to the final of the Scottish FA Cup to face Dundee United. They lifted the trophy

THE CELTIC TEAM CELEBRATE VICTORY AFTER THE TENNENT'S SCOTTISH CUP FINAL BETWEEN CELTIC AND DUNDEE UNITED AT HAMPDEN PARK ON MAY 28, 2005

after winning 1-0, making O'Neill the most successful manager after Jock Stein, with three league titles, three Scottish Cups, and a League Cup.

Whoever came in to fill the vacancy left by O'Neill would need to be made of reinforced concrete and show his credentials immediately or he would be dead in the water. Gordon Strachan was the man chosen for the job, and he was already up to his neck in July when Celtic folded to a 5-0 defeat in Europe. When they wasted a 3-1 lead in the first game of the new season to come away from Motherwell with a 4-4 draw, there were thunderclaps of discontent.

3RD OCTOBER 2007 SCOTT MCDONALD CELEBRATES AFTER SCORING THE WINNING GOAL DURING THEIR UEFA GROUP D CHAMPIONS LEAGUE MATCH AGAINST AC MILAN

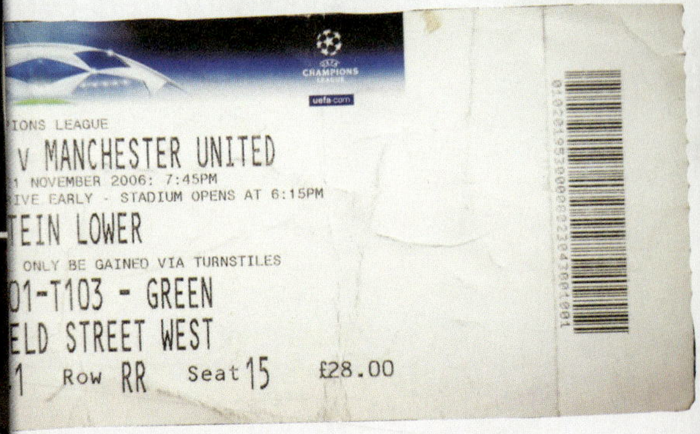

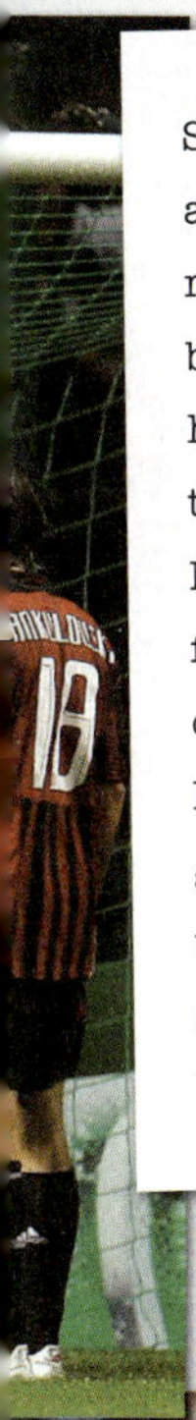

Strachan's problem was that he had inherited an ageing team and one that was still without a true replacement for the glittering Larsson. And the board wished for a reduction in the wage bill; not happy news for a new manager. Strachan rose to the challenge and created his own record to prove he was in no one's shadow. Celtic became the fastest team to reach the SFL championship ever, clinched at the beginning of April 2006 against Heart of Midlothian, 1-0. It came during a nineteen-game undefeated run, ended ironically by Hearts at the end of April, 3-0. Not that a loss was of any significance by then. Hearts were second in the table behind Celtic, who had romped home with 91 points.

And they had the League Cup safely tucked under their shirts by then, too. They had beaten Falkirk, Rangers and Motherwell to meet Dunfermline in the final, which they dominated, coming away with a 3-0 victory. (They had beaten them 8-1 in the league.) Another Double; not bad for Strachan's first season in charge. The doubters had been well and truly silenced; if not entirely satisfied.

What could be pulled out of the bag for the 2006-07 season. Players such as Hartson, Agathe, Mulgrew and Sutton left the club, ten of them in all, to make room for younger players. Jiří Jarošík, Jan Vennegoor of Hesselink, and later Paul Hartley became Celtic men.

Celtic started off well, apart from losing to Hearts 1-2 in the second match. From there, they went on a twenty-seven-game undefeated run that took them to a second league consecutive championship. They dominated the league to such an extent that losing five of the last nine games couldn't trip them up. They claimed the title on the 22nd of April 2007 after a 2-1 win against Kilmarnock in which Nakamura scored with a twenty-five yard free kick in the final minute.

There was a Double for the second consecutive season; the Scottish Cup came their way when they beat Dunfermline for the second time in a cup final, this time the Scottish FA Cup final, 1-0. There was less good news in the League Cup where they had lost on penalties to Falkirk in the quarter-final, and in Europe, a meeting against AC Milan in round two of the UEFA Cup was the end of the road in that competition. That had been Celtic's first time in the last sixteen; so a success on that level, at least.

JAN VENNEGOOR OF HESSELINK IS ECSTATIC AFTER SCORING ON HIS CELTIC DEBUT, AUGUST 26 2006

Captain Neil Lennon left at the end of the season after 301 appearances. Stephen McManus now took over the captaincy.

On November the 7th, John Reid became chairman instead of Brian Quinn, who had been in the chair for seven years. Scott McDonald and Massimo Donati came to Celtic Park to help Strachan bring more silverware to the club in the 2007-08 season as the team chased a third league title. By the middle of March 2008 that was the one honour that they could still claim, because the Scottish League Cup, Scottish FA Cup, and European Champions League challenges had come to nothing. They got revenge on AC Milan in Europe, but they couldn't get past Barcelona, losing 2-4 on aggregate. It had been a tough fight.

March ended with more bad news; a loss to fellow challengers for the league title Rangers, 0-1. Celtic were now six points behind their Glasgow rivals. It looked hopeless.

Yet when the teams met again in April, Celtic had started on a seven-game undefeated run and Rangers were at the receiving end of the sting that downed them 2-1. A spectacular Nakamura goal from thirty yards had given Celtic the lead, and despite a missed penalty, Jan Vennegoor of Hesselink's goal in injury time cancelled out Novo's equaliser for Rangers. Rangers went down yet again, 3-2, on the twenty-seventh of the month. Celtic met Dundee United in the last game of the season as league leaders, and the 1-0 win was enough; Strachan had guided Celtic to three successive league titles, the third manager to do so after Willie Maley and Jock Stein.

There was a tinge of sadness, too, for Tommy Burns, former player and manager had died earlier that week of skin cancer. People remembered former Celtic player Phil O'Donnell, as well. The Motherwell player had collapsed and died in December 2007.

There is no doubt that Strachan's magic brew lost its flavour somewhat after that even though Paddy McCourt, Marc Crosas and Georgios Samaras were now all stirring away vigorously.

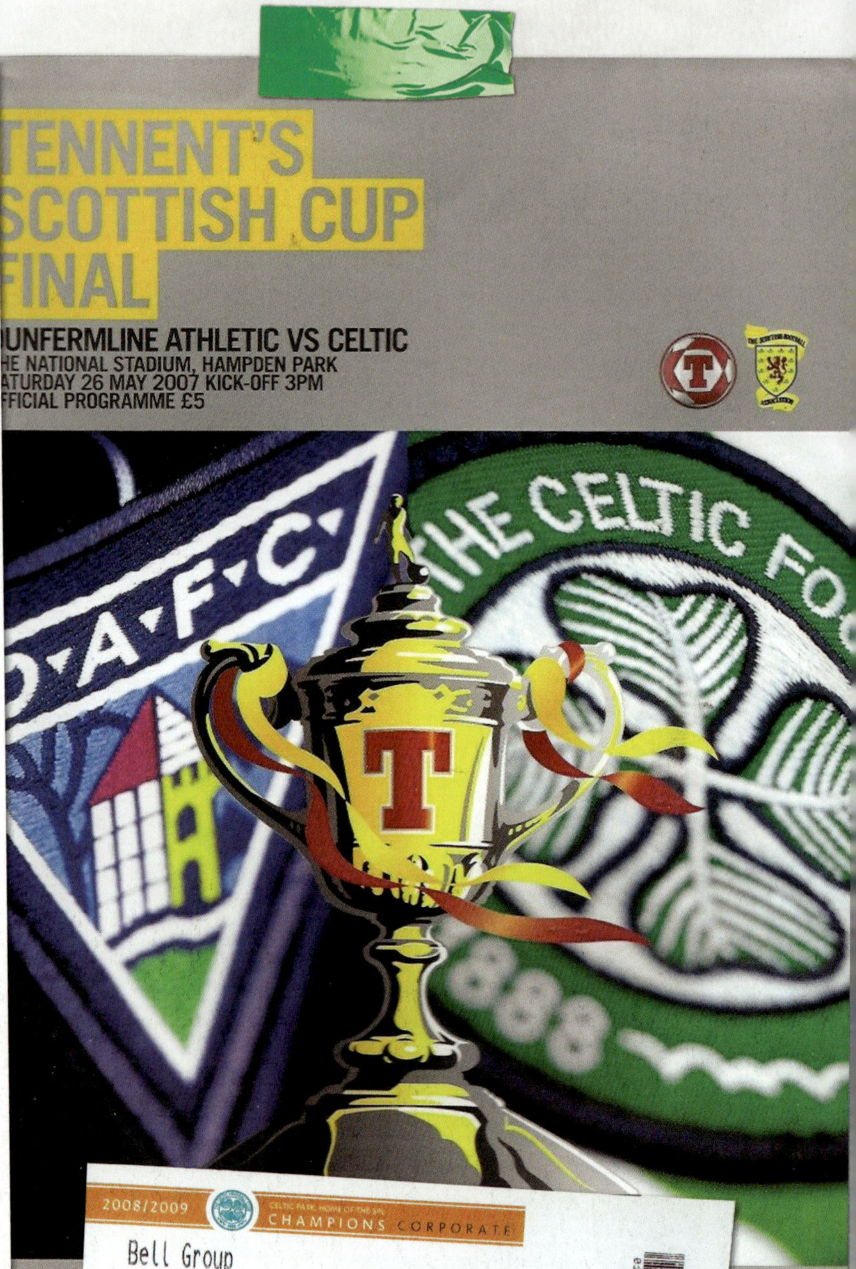

Celtic were top of the league table for much of the 2008-09 season, but the second half was plagued with dropped points, and they eventually paid the price, losing the title to Rangers by four points having been able to beat them only once. But at least there had been a 2-0 win against the Huns in the Scottish League Cup final in March 2009, to look back on with pleasure. O'Dea and McGeady had put the fans out of their misery with two goals in extra time. And St. Mirren had been squashed in a glorious 7-0 game in February 2009. Slim pickings, nonetheless, for a club used to Doubles.

Strachan decided to call it a day after four years, and handed over the reigns to Tony Mowbray on the 16th June 2009.

Mowbray hardly had time to unpack before he was gone again.

He was sacked in March 2010; Celtic had been unable to break a run of poor performances that had seen all the Cup challenges go up in smoke before the finals even came in sight. The 4-0 defeat to St. Mirren on the 24th March abruptly ended Mowbray's Celtic career. Scott McDonald had gone too, and Robbie Keane was now the torchbearer; he became the top goal scorer with 16. That low tally just about said it all.

Neil Lennon took over to try and salvage the season. Lennon presided over an amazing turn around on the field; Rangers were beaten 2-1 during a run of eight games without defeat to the end of the season. Sadly, it was too late to take the title.

Nothing had helped, and for the first time since 2003, Celtic came out of a season empty-handed.

But Lennon had brought hope, at least.

15TH MARCH 2009 CELTIC CELEBRATE VICTORY AFTER THE CIS INSURANCE CUP FINAL BETWEEN RANGERS AND CELTIC

A BLAZE

Lennon was named as the new manager. The revolving door ushered out McGeady, McManus and Boruc among others in the summer of 2010; Crosas left later in the season. Gary Hooper came in, and promptly took over the top goal scorer spot for the next three seasons.

Lennon's first full season was filled with excitement and two finals.

The Bhoys began where they had left off, and roared away to eight games without defeat, coming unstuck against Rangers, 1-3 in October. Knocked off balance, it took them until December to get back to the top spot. Rangers had a fight on their hands. Hopes in the UEFA Europa League and the UEFA Champions League were dashed early on, but the Scottish League Cup run brought them through to a final against Rangers. Celtic had already eliminated Rangers from the Scottish Cup in the fifth round, when Lennon had managed to get himself a four-match ban for an argument with Rangers' manager Ally McCoist. Celtic lost the League Cup final 2-1.

As the final month came around, Celtic were second in the table. A fatal stumble against Inverness, 2-3 meant that the title would depend on Rangers losing their last game... which they didn't, and so won the title by one point.

Six days later, Celtic were in the Scottish Cup final against Motherwell, whom they had beaten 4-0 in the final game of the league season.

Lennon was able to claim his first cup when three goals went in for Celtic. Celtic's Ki-Sung-Yueng was man of the match, and he and Mulgrew took the honours with a goal apiece either side of a Motherwell own goal by Stephen Craigan, a deflection of a Mark Wilson shot.

21ST MAY 2011 NEIL LENNON AFTER HIS TEAM WON THE SCOTTISH CUP FINAL AGAINST MOTHERWELL

It was a wonderful way to end a season that had seen also seen Rangers decisively beaten twice, 3-0 and 2-0. It was also a strong answer to the abhorrent campaign of terror that had been waged against Lennon. Bombs and bullets had been sent to him on separate occasions, and he had also been physically attacked.

Celtic's 2011-12 league year got off to a shaky start in which only seven of the first twelve games were won. It took until November for a twenty-one game undefeated run to kick in and put them on top of the

OF GLORY

table, a position they did not relinquish again. Rangers were beaten twice and third-placed Motherwell four times. Celtic were playing wonderful football, and signed off with a 5-0 hammering of Heart of Midlothian; although that couldn't make up for the defeat suffered in the Scottish FA Cup semi-final when Hearts beat them 1-2.

But once they had flattened Kilmarnock 6-0 in April 2012, the League Championship had been theirs, and would have been even if Rangers had not had ten points deducted because they had gone into liquidation. As it was, Celtic had 93 points to Rangers 73. Lennon's Celtic were back on top.

In an extraordinary season, the fate that Celtic had only narrowly avoided struck Rangers; they went into liquidation. Newly reformed, the club was placed in the Third Division, a terrible fate for a club of such standing.

20TH FEBRUARY 2011 SCOTT BROWN & KYLE BARTLEY OF RANGERS SHOW THEIR PASSION

21ST MAY 2011 CELTIC CELEBRATE WINNING THE SCOTTISH CUP AGAINST MOTHERWELL

7TH NOVEMBER 2012 JOE LEDLEY TAKES ON LIONEL MESSI IN THE UEFA CHAMPIONS LEAGUE GROUP G MATCH

Celtic successfully retained the league title in the 2012-13 season; although their form was patchy they were on the top spot most of the time and they eventually pulled sixteen points clear of Motherwell to take the title with 79 points. And if there was no glory in the Scottish League Cup or in Europe - despite a magnificent game against Barcelona in which the Spanish side went down 2-1 - the gleam of glittering silverware came in the shape of the Scottish FA Cup to complete another FA Cup/League Cup Double. It was achieved with a 3-0 victory over Hibernian. What a fitting tribute to an old Celtic star who had passed away in January of that year, Sean Fallon.

Gary Hooper and Kelvin Wilson were the losses that year, bemoaned by fans. Virgil van Dijk came to try and cheer them up.

Like Dr. Who, the Scottish league went through another of its periodic transformations and emerged as the Scottish Premiership.

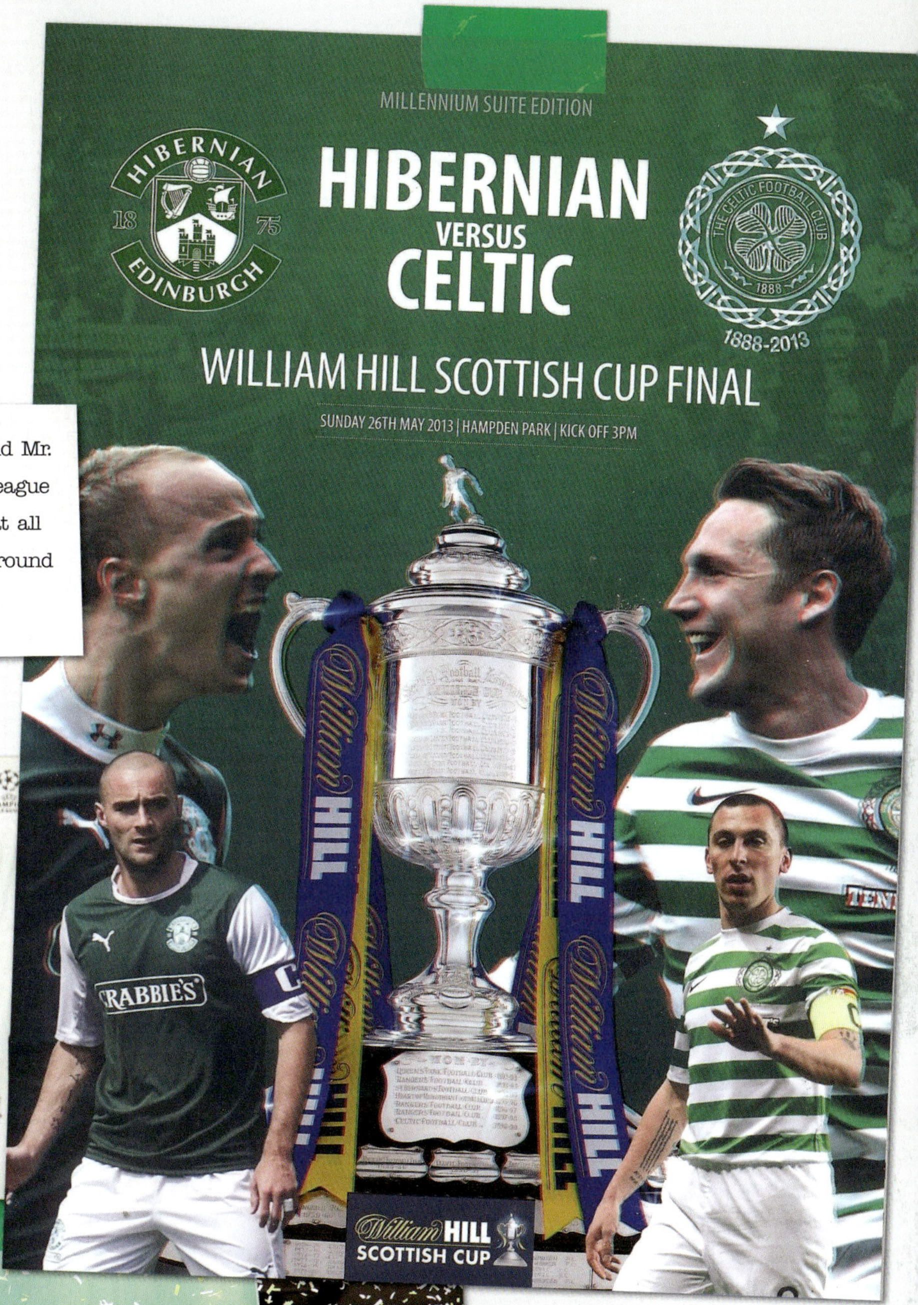

For Celtic, a more apt comparison would be Dr. Jekyll and Mr. Hyde, because the cup challenges were as awful as the league challenge was wonderful. There was barely a challenge at all in the Scottish Cup and the League Cup; round five and round three. Awful, therefore.

26TH MAY 2013 THE BHOYS CELEBRATE WITH THE TROPHY AFTER DEFEATING HIBERNIAN 3-0 AT HAMPDEN STADIUM

In the league, on the other hand, there was just one defeat as Celtic romped home with 99 points, 29 ahead of Motherwell. The title was won on the 26th of March, the earliest date since the 1928-29 season. Another terrific record for the Bhoys. It was the 45th league title, Celtic's third in a row; a memorable way to celebrate the club's 125th season of competitive football. Kris Commons was top goal scorer with 32 followed by Anthony Stokes on 21, in a season that saw Motherwell, Aberdeen and Dundee United beaten three times each.

Disappointing news came at the end of the season; the man who had steered the club to three league titles, Neil Lennon, decided that after four years as manager, the time had come to move on.

Celtic headed off into their 126th year of competitive football with uncertainty tugging at their heels. There were doubts about the new manager's ability to steer a team of Celtic's stature, and the newspapers were soon working up a great sweat with reports that Ronny Deila was "weak" or "a puppet". Losing the final four pre-season friendlies didn't help either.

Georgios Samaras had moved on to West Brom and new faces arrived; the Swedish player John Guidetti, on loan from Manchester City, Stuart Armstrong and Gary Mackay-Steven both from Dundee. All three would soon be rising up the goal-scoring tables.

Any wobbles in the fans' stomachs were eased by a 3-0 win against St Johnstone in the first game of the season and a 6-1 thrashing of Dundee United a week later.

In a repeat meeting of the previous year, Celtic met Inverness CT in the third game. Then, they had managed a draw at home. This year they lost by a single goal. Was this the moment everyone had predicted, when the team would fall apart?

Well, write off a Celtic team only if you like humble pie. The naysayers soon had to eat enough to fill an elephant.

Still, it was Inverness CT who were to prove the stumbling block later in the season, too, tipping Celtic out of the Scottish Cup in the semi-final (a better run than the previous season, nonetheless) with a 3-2 victory. And whilst we are at it, we might as well get the rest of the gloom out of the way first; the UEFA Champions League was lost in the play-off round to NK Maribor 0-1, also in that first month of August.

Back in the league there was the first of two home defeats to cope with. 1-0 in October against Hamilton Academical. A second came in March 2015 against St. Johnstone, 1-0.

It was, then, a mighty relief that the team suddenly found their feet and romped off to a run of eight games without defeat in which Ross County, 5-0, and St Mirren, 4-1, suffered the most. There was also revenge against Inverness CT with a 1-0 victory at home thanks to a Guidetti goal in the 48th minute, plus a satisfying 2-1 defeat of hot contenders for the league title, Aberdeen.

o why they then lost to Dundee United 2-1 and drew against Ross County in back to back games is anyone's guess.

hankfully that aberration passed and in the next run of games they came back with a vengeance scoring 4-0 victories n three matches against Motherwell, Hamilton and Aberdeen again.

n March came the thrilling moment that everyone had hoped vould arrive; winning the first big competition of the season. The team ran out against Dundee United in the League Cup inal on the 15th March 2015, and when they left the pitch hey were the League Cup holders with a 2-0 win.

By the beginning of May the league title was in the bag with second-placed Aberdeen a long way back on points. Saving he best till last, Celtic romped home in a 5-0 hammering of Dundee and then took down second-placed Aberdeen - again - or good measure, with two games to go, 1-0 at home.

Despite that, you can never have enough of a good thing after all, everyone was waiting for that last home game against Inverness CT so that the earlier humiliation could be

24TH MAY 2015 CELTIC GET A GUARD OF HONOUR FROM THE INVERNESS TEAM AT AT CELTIC PARK

wiped off the slate with a decisive victory to end a wonderful season for the club and its new manager. The lads had already turned in a run of 10 undefeated games heading to that last match, their best run of the season. An 11th game undefeated would be the icing on the cake. So what happened?

Unbelievable!

The Bhoys were out for revenge that day of May 24th 2015 and delivered a tour de force that had Inverness rocked back on the defensive, unable to stop the green and white wave overwhelming them. Let's cut the story short and get to the fun part... Celtic 5 Inverness CT 0. Yes. 5-0, the fairy-tale ending to the season had come true and Celtic had taken the league title in brilliant style. The men who sealed the visitors' fate as Celtic romped home - even being denied an obvious penalty - were Šćepović on the 5th and 70th, Johansen on the 18th, Griffiths on the 80th and Kris Commons on the 90th minute.

So ended a cracking first season for Ronnie Deila, and with his Bhoys triumphant, one that gave enormous encouragement for the future. Top goalscorer was Leigh Griffiths, who really plugged himself in bringing his tally up from 7 in the 2013/14 season to 20 this year, with John Guidetti and Kris Commons on his heels with 15 and 16 each. 92 points in total leaving Aberdeen far behind on 75 and only 17 goals conceded with an 11-game undefeated run to end the season.

Any Celtic fan who was unhappy that day must have been kidnapped by aliens without a TV licence.

Having romped home in 2014 for their third consecutive league title, it was difficult to see who was going to knock them off that perch in the 2015/16 season.

It transpired that no one was, not even Aberdeen, even though they had another good season chomping at Celtic's heels and got closer to them this time, but only because the Celtic points count slipped from the glorious 96 of the previous season, to 86. There were rumblings of discontent.

MOUSSA DEMBELE TACKLES KENNY MILLER OF RANGERS DURING THE LADBROKES SCOTTISH PREMIER LEAGUE MATCH AT CELTIC PARK, 10TH SEPTEMBER 2016

Nonetheless, Celtic began well with a run of six games without defeat. Although their form improved as the season progressed, they lost four again as they had done the previous season. There was a 12-game undefeated run from December 2015 through to May 2016, but their drawn games count went up to eight. Not enough, damage though, to give anyone else any hope.

That man Leigh Griffiths was top goalscorer once more, this time with a sizzling 40 goals, double his previous season's tally. That made Griffiths the highest scoring player since the days of the legendary Henrik Larsson.

Yes, it was disappointing that no cups had been won at home or abroad despite reaching the semis in the League and Scottish Cup finals. And yes, it was more than disappointing that they were defeated by Rangers in the Scottish Cup semi-final. So, Ronny Deila decided that it was time for him to move on. But he was leaving after a blistering farewell against Motherwell when the Bhoys hurled 7 into the Motherwell net. The fans had seen 6 and then later, 5 go in against Dundee and even 8 against Hamilton Academical. They had much to thank Ronny Deila for another league title, for a start, their fifth in a row.

But now it was up the new man in charge to make sure that the Celtic fire was stoked once more. The choice fell on Northern Irish manager Brendan Rodgers. Brendan Rodgers had been in charge at Watford and Liverpool, so that looked promising.

Well, 'promising' turned out to be a slight understatement!

Putting the cart before the horse - because it's such a terrific achievement it deserves immediate mention - when did anyone last enjoy a season where the Scottish lads were undefeated through to the end of the year!? Yes, a clean sheet with just four games drawn. An astonishing feat. And what scores as the Bhoys ran riot through the opposition; Rivals Rangers were blown off the field completely, 5-1 in September 2016, with Moussa Dembélé creating history by whacking in a hat-trick, the first that Celtic had scored in an Old Firm fixture; poor Kilmarnock crumbled 6-1, and previous season's league runners up Aberdeen were sunk at home. 1-0, to go nicely with the 4-1 defeat Celtic had dealt them at home in August 2016. It would not be the last.

And then the cup jinx was broken when, on the 27th of November, Celtic lifted the Scottish League Cup after facing Aberdeen again and coming through decisive 3-0 victors.

By January of 2017, Rangers were lagging 19 points behind Celtic. It was shaping up to be a cracking year for the Hoops.

MOUSSA DEMBELE SCORES HIS 2ND GOAL DURING THE LADBROKES SCOTTISH PREMIERSHIP MATCH AGAINST RANGERS ON 10TH SEPTEMBER 2016

They entered the new year Scottish Cup competition knocking Inverness CT for six, literally, and seeing off Rangers again, 2-0, with a superb finish from Callum McGregor and a penalty from Scott Sinclair securing another cup final appearance, where those tigers from Aberdeen would be waiting hungrily for a victim, and Celtic would be looking to complete the domestic clean sweep, their first since 2001.

As the year progressed, Celtic dispensed with one team after the other in an astonishing display, slowing only in March for their first draw since September of the previous year, as Rangers shared the goals in a 1-1 scoreline. Partick 1-1 and Ross County 2-2, managed the same feat. Hearts, however, got the 5-0 treatment as Celtic secured the league title, and Rangers might have thought that they were in with a chance when the sides met again in April; they were soon disabused of that silly notion, hammered again 5-1, their heaviest defeat at Ibrox since 1915. A penalty, a header, a curling drive beat them down as Scott Sinclair, Leigh Griffiths (a spectacular drive), Callum McGregor and Dedryck Boyata swept the ball into the Rangers' net.

A final game of the season resulted in a 2-0 victory over Hearts; Celtic took their 6th consecutive league title, a truly magnificent achievement – the best since that incredible period in the 1960s and early 1970s when they won nine consecutive league titles. Before that, you have to go back to 1910 when they also hamstered away six consecutive titles. And what's more, they had completed the season undefeated, the first Scottish side to achieve this in the top-flight since 1899. An incredible debut for Brendan Rodgers. Celtic's 106 points left Aberdeen trailing in the distance on 76.

With the Double under their hoops, the team went into the cup final arena on the 27th of May.

And the records were about to be beaten again.

In what turned out to be a scintillating game, Aberdeen went ahead after just nine minutes. Shock turned to joy, though, as Stuart Armstrong whacked in the equaliser just two minutes later. And there's a very good reason why the Celtic lads are champions, and as the game wore on they asserted their dominance and piled on the pressure to be rewarded with a Rogic winner late in stoppage time. 2-1.

What an extraordinary team, what an extraordinary climax, to a stunning season. The 37th time the Hoops had taken the world's oldest national football trophy; the first clean sweep in 16 years, undefeated in the entire domestic season, a feat unequalled in Scottish football history!

Moussa Dembélé was the 2017 man with the magic boots, top goalscorer with 32 to his credit, which included

three hat-tricks; against Rangers, St Johnstone and Inverness CT.

WILLIAM HILL SCOTTISH CUP FINAL AGAINST ABERDEEN, CELTIC'S TOM ROGIC CELEBRATES HIS LATE WINNER, MAY 27 2017

CELTIC

With a domestic treble under their boots for the first time since the 2000-01 season, and having lashed Rangers with their heaviest defeat at Ibrox since 1915, 5-1, Celtic set out into the new season of 2017-18 with confidence high and a team that could perform extraordinary displays of football. And the future was beyond what anyone could have expected. It would be wonderful, wouldn't it, if the Bhoys could achieve a domestic double at least? Well, a treble would be even better, wouldn't it? Ah.

With the same feared forwards, Leigh Griffiths, Moussa Dembélé and Odsonne Édouard back for the new season, fifteen games without defeat was a thundering start to the season and Celtic thundered four past Heart of Midlothian (let's forget that they thundered in 4 against Celtic in December) Ross County, Saint Johnstone, and 5 past Motherwell. No one could complain about that start. Scott Sinclair was usually around somewhere to finish a move, and, indeed, he finished the season top goalscorer with 18.

By December, had Celtic already secured the League Cup trophy with a 2-0 defeat of Motherwell in the final. Runners up for top goalscorer, Moussa Dembélé and James Forrest, were Motherwell's downfall in that contest.

On the 13th of May 2018, Celtic finished the league season by losing at home. But by then they had already won the Scottish Premiership title, 83 points to Aberdeen's 73, so that last-day result was neither here nor there. And there it was, the second domestic double in a row.

But the lads had one final ace up their sleeves; the Scottish Cup final against pesky Motherwell. As Motherwell had already proven themselves to be dangerous opponents, nothing could be taken for granted. Nothing, that is, except the boots of midfielders Callum McGregor and Olivier Ntcham. Callum struck after eleven minutes with a goal that had to be seen to be believed. Leaping onto the ball as it was headed

SCOTT BROWN AND TEAM MATES CELEBRATE WITH THE TROPHY AFTER THE BETFRED CUP FINAL AGAINST ABERDEEN AT HAMPDEN PARK, DECEMBER 2, 2018

out from the defence, he slipped through the pincer movement by two defenders and sent an absolute scorcher, an unstoppable shot, into the net.

On the twenty-fifth minute, Olivier followed suit. Superb Celtic play saw Dembélé hold off the defence before sending the pass to Olivier, who fired the second low into the net. It was all over for Motherwell. Celtic, on the other hand, had achieved an incredible treble in two subsequent seasons. A double treble no less!

And how do you top that?

Well, we're talking about Celtic FC, here, so the way you top it is to repeat it and see if the experience tastes as good the third time.

Upon entering their 130th season of competitive football for the 2018-19 season, Celtic had raised their fans' expectation to hitherto unknown heights.

Sadly, the unique Moussa Dembélé couldn't take any more excitement and left the club to join Lyon, where life was bound to be quieter. But men of the calibre of Griffiths, Édouard (who had had such a good season whilst on loan the previous season and now transferred to the club to become top goalscorer with 23 to his credit), Sinclair or Ntcham were going to have yet another bite at the cherry. The games could begin.

And the league began with a bit of a seesaw, it has to be said, with only three games won from the first six. Now it

was Rangers who proved to be a bit of a pain in the neck and won two of their matches against Celtic, taking away 1-0 and 2-0 victories against their Glasgow rivals; Celtic also took two victories away from the derbies, 1-0 and 2-1. Rangers' effort were to no avail, it must be added, as Celtic still took the league title with 87 points to Rangers' 78, having lost just one of the final eighteen matches. The bulk of the damage to opposing teams was done by the sharpshooting of Édouard, Sinclair and Forrest, with another midfielder, Ryan Christie, claiming the fourth top goalscorer spot with eleven.

Worth mentioning that Celtic had three games where they struck five times during this season, against Dundee, Kilmarnock and Heart of Midlothian. Spare a thought, too, for poor old St Johnstone, who were given the complete runaround as they drowned under the six-goal onslaught. Forrest had a field day, which seems like a mixed metaphor, scoring his hat-trick plus another one for good measure all before the first half had ended, four goals in thirty minutes. Delightful Celtic play and team work brought the desired results, and even a terrible attack that hacked Forrest off his feet couldn't stop the hooped wave.

Nor could anyone stop them from taking yet another domestic trophy when they claimed the Scottish League Cup in December against Aberdeen, 1-0. Ryan Christie did the honours on that occasion.

And then, in February 2019, Manager Brendan Rodgers was suddenly gone.

Which brought about the return of Neil Lennon to the manager's seat that he had vacated in 2014, to try and continue the success story.

Well, just in case anyone still doubted that Celtic was simply unbeatable that season, they roared into the Scottish Cup final against Heart of Midlothian to get revenge for the 1-0 league defeat.

Hearts were in Celtic mouths when their opponents held the team to a 0-0 at half-time, proving that they were not to be underestimated. And they made that crystal clear on the 52nd minute when Celtic failed to clear the area and Edwards put the Hoops 1-0 down as a punishment.

MICHAEL JOHNSTON OF CELTIC DURING THE WILLIAM HILL SCOTTISH CUP FINAL BETWEEN HEART OF MIDLOTHIAN AND CELTIC AT HAMPDEN PARK, MAY 25, 2019

Celtic then went into top gear and showed why they were the best team in the land. The fight back began, and when Édouard was caught in a sandwich and brought down in the penalty area. Hearts were in trouble as Édouard put away the penalty. And then... oh, what a brilliant Celtic moment when a superb header found Monsieur Édouard tearing forward into in a prairie of space and with a gorgeous lob over the goalie put in number two on 82 minutes. Celtic had achieved an incredible triple treble.

The standards that Celtic had set over the past three years seemed almost too great for anyone to emulate. There would need to be a team of the quality of Celtic to do it. There was. That team was called Celtic. And there was a man of exceptional goalscoring talent in that team; Odsonne Édouard, who would rise to become top goalscorer for three season in a row.

Another record-breaking year for Celtic started off in the league in 2019 with an even harsher thrashing of poor St Johnstone, who vanished from sight with a 7-0 defeat that began in the ninth minute and from which Ryan Christie took home a hat-trick.

There were just two defeats that season, one to Livingston (anyone heard of them?) and Rangers, 2-1. Any hopes that team had that they had managed to turn the tables on the Hoops was short lived, because they went down to Celtic in the Scottish League Cup 1-0, and Celtic romped home to a ninth-in-a-row league title that season with 80 points to Rangers' 67, absolutely demolishing a whole host of clubs on the way to doing so. Ross County 6-0, Motherwell 5-2, Livingston 4-0, Motherwell 4-0, Heart of Midlothian and St Mirren 5-0 each game.

All that stood between Celtic and their fourth treble was the Scottish Cup final against Heart of Midlothian.

What a match that had both teams fighting toe to toe throughout. It was touch and go for the Glasgow Bhoys, but they weren't giving up on the dream and produced the fight of their lives.

A glorious goal by Christie set Celtic off on the right foot as he picked up a bad defensive clearance to send the ball sailing into the net from outside the penalty area. The lead increased to two after Édouard put away another penalty.

On 48 minutes Hearts came back to life and took back one goal, equalising on the 67th.

It was left to Conor Hazard to save the day with a fabulous penalty save and then it was Celtic's turn to re-establish superiority with a Griffith goal tapped in after a rocket Brown header just failed to find the net.

But with a third by Hearts making it 3-3 at full-time, the dreaded penalty shoot-out had arrived. Christie missed his chance, but Connor Hazard, playing for just the third time, was the saviour of the day with two wonderful saves. Celtic had made the impossible possible and achieved the fourth triple in subsequent seasons, the quadruple triple. What a magnificent,

unparalleled achievement!

CELTIC'S ODSONNE EDOUARD (LEFT) CELEBRTAES WITH SCOTT BROWN (CENTRE) AND MOHAMED ELYOUNOUSSI DURING THE WILLIAM HILL SCOTTISH CUP FINAL BETWEEN CELTIC AND HEARTS AT HAMPDEN PARK, ON DECEMBER 20, 2020

CELTIC CAPTAIN SCOTT BROWN LIFTS THE 2019/2020 SCOTTISH CUP DURING THE WILLIAM HILL SCOTTISH CUP FINAL BETWEEN CELTIC AND HEARTS AT HAMPDEN PARK, ON DECEMBER 20, 2020

A NEW

I suppose that after such success, the team can be forgiven for taking time out, or rather, a season out. Yet the team had started out well in Au-gust 2020 with a nine-game undefeated run. Then it all went sideways and the draws piled up accompanied by five league losses. Suddenly, Olivier Ntcham was gone. Absolutely nothing to be done; and Neil Lennon took his hat and departed in February 2021 handing over the reins to John Kennedy for him to guide the team's fortunes - misfortunes would be more appropriate, as the club failed to bring home any silverware for the first time since 2010 - until the end of the season. The Scottish League Cup run had ended in November 2020. Something of a record in itself. In April 2021 the Scottish Cup hope went west, too, as Rangers took home a 2-0 victory. Celtic finished second in the Premiership.

When August 2021 dawned, the Celtic side was a changed beast. Greek-born Angelos Postecoglou was now manager, presiding over a new forward lineup. Ryan Christie and Odsonne Édouard would go. Young blood Karamoko Dembélé was still there, as were McGregor, Sinclair and Forrest. Scott Brown was no longer commander of the midfield men, though.

Angelous Postecoglou was not the only new addition. Winger João Pedro Neves Filipe, Jota to the fans, was on loan from Benfica, and two forwards had joined the team who were to prove their worth in glorious style; Japa-nese player Kyogo Furuhashi, and Georgios Giakoumakis, both 27 years of age. Kyogo would garner a tally of 20 goals in 33 appearances making him top goalscorer and Georgios wasn't far behind with 17 in 29 outings.

At first, it seemed as though the team was suffering teething problems. Of the first seven games they won just three. Was this the stuff of champions, the fans asked. As it turned out the answer was yes. Two of those wins were 6-0 goal feasts against Dundee and St Mirren and fans were treated to the same spectacle on the last game of the season when 6 went past Motherwell. Both Georgios and Kyogo scored two apiece in that one with

CELTIC'S KYOGO FURUHASHI IS AT CELTIC PARK ON AUGUST 02, 2021

Jota and midfielder David Turnbull adding the other two. By then, Celtic had not lost another game; a 32-match unbeaten run. The most goals in one game were scored against St Johnstone when 7 hit the opposition net. The most satisfying win was without doubt the game against Rangers in February 2022, in which Celtic smacked their Glasgow opponents 3-0.

Unfortunately, Celtic couldn't quite make it to the Scottish Cup final, but by the end of the season they had claimed a domestic double by taking the Premiership title, having won the Scottish League Cup in December of 2021, 2-1 against old upstarts Hibernian with Kyogo Furuhashi getting both goals.

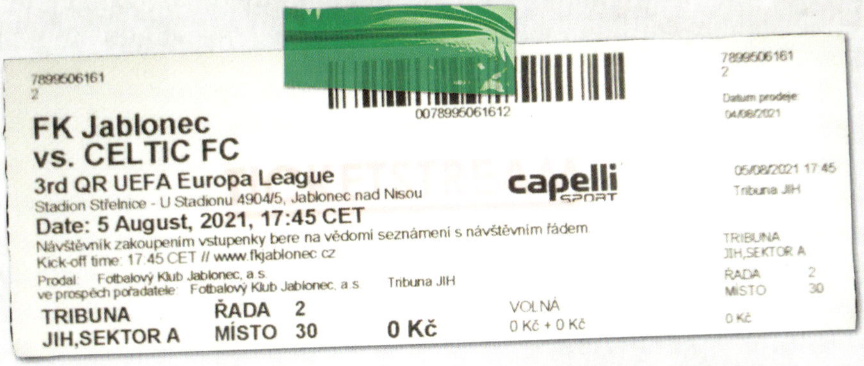

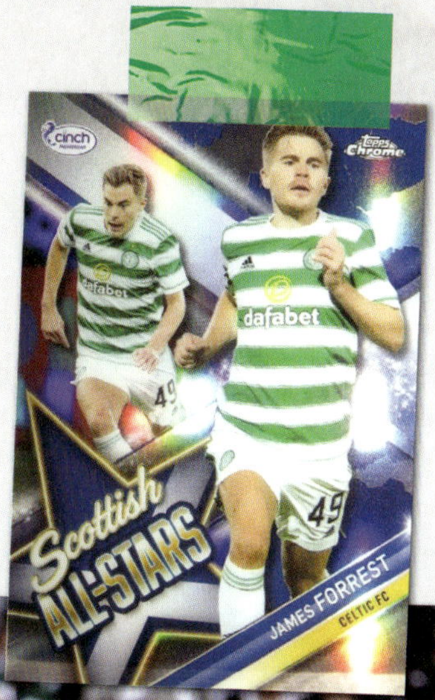

CELTIC FC HUDDLE UP AHEAD OF THE UEFA EUROPA LEAGUE PLAY-OFFS LEG ONE MATCH BETWEEN CELTIC FC AND AZ ALKMAAR AT ON AUGUST 18, 2021

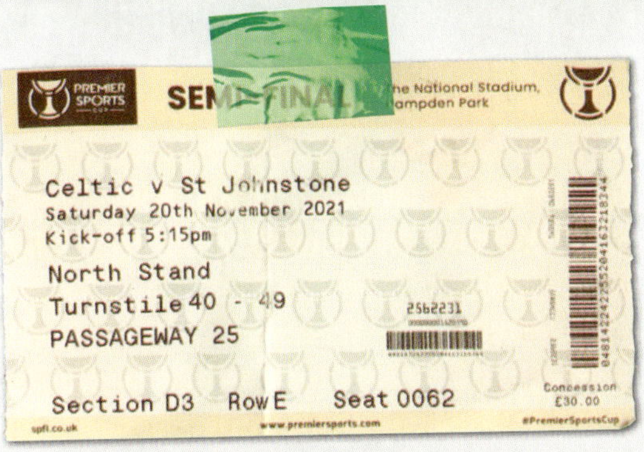

DECADE

What a see-saw game that was with Celtic firing in chances but failing to get the ball into the net only to see their efforts rewarded with a Hibernian goal. But champions withstand such setbacks with steel resolve and Celtic waves moved forwards dangerously until a superb pass through the Hibernian defence to Kyogo, who sped through into the box and drove a low ball past the keeper, rectified the deficit on the 51st minute. And then 20 minutes later another fabulous pass split the defence once more and there he was again, Kyogo, to lob a brilliantly weighted ball into the net for a well-deserved Celtic victory.

The Hoops finished the league season in true style giving fans a 6-goal delicacy to savour against hapless Motherwell. Furuhashi and Giakoumakis popped in two apiece (and were, therefore, season's top goalscorer and second best goalscorer with 20 and 17 respectively) aided and abetted by Turnbull and Jota on an afternoon of joyous football delights.

Kyogo was on sparkling form, razor-sharp and performed a twist and whip for the starting goal with Turnbull executing neat ball control to push in the second. Kyogo, ever watchful, was still running forwards as the ball descended in front of him and he drove home a volley for the third, a true master of the ball. Then it was Jota's turn to sweep in the fourth, followed by Giakoumakis claiming his first with an overhead kick and his second in added time.

Celtic were well and truly back on top.

Celebration then, but also tears of farewell as midfielder, Australian Tom Rogic left the field for the last time. After 178 appearances, Rogic had been faithful to the club since 2013 and deserved his standing ovation. His teammate Nir Bitton, another faithful since 2013, had also played his last game for the Hoops.

So emotions ran over as captain Callum McGregor lifted the cup to bring to an end another magnificent season for a team with a unique place in Scottish football history.

CALLUM MCGREGOR CELEBRATES WITH THE CUP AFTER VICTORY IN THE PREMIER SPORTS CUP FINAL AGAINST HIBERNIAN, HAMPDEN PARK, DECEMBER 19 2021

Celtic can look back proudly on a magnificent, indeed uniquely successful history since they ran out for their first league game on the 23rd of August 1890 against Heart of Midlothian. (A 5-0 victory by the way!)

There have been more than a fair share of disappointments and trials, but the club has overcome them all to rise to triumphant heights. The Bhoys have ridden the storms, refused to be downhearted, and are now dominating the top echelons of Scottish football once more. Celtic are riding high, and can confidently look forward to the future, and supporters can expect more exciting games filled with the thrilling, and occasionally unexpected, football for the which the Bhoys are known. They have seen some of the most talented players in football wear the hooped shirts and make the club one of the greatest in the world.

THE PLAYERS

ANY LIST CLAIMING TO NAME THE BEST PLAYERS WILL INEVITABLY RUN THE RISK OF FALLING SHORT IN THE ESTIMATION OF MANY READERS, AND CELTIC HAS HAD A HOST OF EXCEPTIONAL TALENTS. HERE, HOWEVER, IS A VERY BRIEF RUNDOWN OF SOME CELTIC PLAYERS WHO WERE OUTSTANDING FOR A VARIETY OF REASONS.

KENNY DALGLISH

Kenneth Mathieson "Kenny" Dalglish, was born on the 4th of March 1951 in Glasgow, Scotland. His first school was Milton bank primary school where he began playing football as a goalkeeper. He signed for Celtic on a provisional contract in 1967, and by 1971 he was established in the first-team. He won four Scottish Cups, one Scottish League Cup, and four Scottish First Division titles with the club, before signing for Liverpool in 1977. By then, he had appeared for Celtic 320 times and scored 167 goals. Dalglish has also been capped 102 times for Scotland scoring 30 goals for the national team. He is considered to have been very creative, a skilled forward, a team player in midfield who could score goals, and a great all-rounder.

In 1999, Dalglish returned to Celtic as Director of Football, and was appointed manager in 2000 after John Barnes was sacked. Despite helping the club to win the Scottish League Cup, his contract was terminated.

On the 26th of November 1974, Dalglish married Marina with whom he has four children, and in 1984 he was awarded an MBE. He won the FWA Footballer of the Year award twice, and the PFA Player of the Year award. He has also been inducted into both the Scottish and the English Football Halls of Fame.

JIMMY JOHNSTONE

James Connolly "Jimmy" Johnstone was born on the 30th of September 1944 in Viewpark, Scotland, and died on the 13th of March 2006 in Uddingston, Scotland.

Johnstone was the youngest of five children, and his first school was St Columba's Primary, where teachers encouraged him to play. He signed for Celtic in 1961, and began his first team career with them on the 23rd of March 1963, remaining with the team until 1975, and notching up 515 appearances. He also won 23 caps for the Scottish national side.

5ft 4in "Jinky", as he was known because of his magical dribbling skills, his masterful sense of balance and his vibrant athleticism, was probably the greatest player ever to grace the Celtic team. Able to turn defenders and sprint out of danger, the outside right was also known as "a man of laughter and joy".

Johnstone was part of the great "Lisbon Lions" team that won the European Cup for Celtic in 1967.

In November 2001, Johnstone received a diagnosis of Motor Neurone disease, and finally succumbed to his illness in March 2006. A bronze, life-size statue of the player stands on the site of his former school in Uddingston.

CHARLIE TULLY

Charles Patrick "Charlie" Tully was born on the 11th of July 1924 in Belfast, Northern Ireland, and died on the 27th of July 1971.

Tully joined Celtic in 1948, and over a career spanning 11 years, he scored 47 goals in 319 matches. He also played ten games for the Northern Ireland team.

Tully quickly earned a reputation as an outstanding footballer, becoming a celebrity, perhaps the first in football, with his name and picture on merchandising. His extraordinary ball skills made him a legend at Celtic, a reputation cemented when he scored a goal from a corner kick, and then repeated the trick when the referee disallowed the goal. His self-assured brilliance with the ball was also coupled with a "happy-go-lucky approach to the game" that seemed to point to a lack of commitment, and which led to frustration in others both on and off the field. Nonetheless, Tully has gone down as one of the greats in Celtic football history.

On the 27th of July 1971, Charlie Tully died in his sleep at home in Belfast. He is survived by his sons Charlie and Brian and his daughter Patricia.

HENRIK LARSSON

Henrik Edward Larsson was born on the 20th of September 1971 in Helsingborg, Sweden.

Larsson's father came from Cape Verde, and instilled a love of football in his son. Larsson junior began his professional career at the age of 17, signing on full-time with Helsingborg in 1992. Larsson moved to Celtic in 1977 after four years with Feyenoord. As a striker, he helped win the club four Scottish League titles, two Scottish League Cups and two Scottish Cups, with his total of 315 appearances netting him 242 goals. He was top goal scorer for Celtic six times, and top goal scorer in the SPL for five of those seasons. Larsson missed most of the 1999-2000 season due to a severe leg break sustained in a match in Lyon, France.

Larsson is a legend at Celtic, revered for his goal scoring abilities, ball skills and ability to deceive defenders. He was part of the team that brought the club to domination in Scottish football, and was greatly respected as a perfect professional both on and off the field. Larsson was capped 106 times for Sweden scoring 37 goals, and was voted the greatest Swedish footballer of all time in 2004.

After leaving Celtic - as the SPL's all-time leading goal scorer at that time, with 158 goals - Larsson moved to Barcelona, and then back to Sweden.

Larsson married Magdalena Spjuth on the 21st of June 1996, having met her when he was 19 years old. The couple have one son and one daughter.

Larsson has been inducted into the Scottish Football Hall of Fame, he won the European Golden Boot in 2001, and was the SFWA Footballer of the Year twice and the SPFA Player's Player of the Year twice. He was awarded the Kings' Medal in 2007.

PAUL MCSTAY

Paul Michael Lyons McStay was born on the 22nd of October 1964 in Hamilton, South Lanarkshire, Scotland.

McStay signed for Celtic in 1981, making his league debut on the 30th of January 1982 against Aberdeen in a 3-1 victory for Celtic. He became club captain in 1990, and retained that position until he retired in 1997 after 515 league appearances. During that time, he helped Celtic to win the league title three times, the League Cup once and the Scottish Cup four times. McStay was also capped 76 times for Scotland.

In 2002, Celtic fans voted him a member of Celtic's greatest ever team, and he was voted SFWA Footballer of the Year and Scottish PFA Player of the Year in 1988.

McStay's talents became apparent early on, and he picked up the nickname "the maestro" as a tribute to his world-class performances. He was described as one of the very best midfielders in Europe, blessed with almost faultless footwork and passing skills, calm elegance, and the ability to read the game well.

In 2010, McStay moved to Sydney, Australia with his family.

DANNY MCGRAIN

Daniel Fergus "Danny" McGrain was born on the 1st of May 1950 in Finnieston, Glasgow, Scotland.

McGrain joined Celtic in May 1967, and although he was a midfielder his abilities meant that he could be used in a variety of roles. Eventually, he established himself in the right-back position. On the 25th of March 1972, he fractured his skull during a match against Falkirk. He made a full recovery, and by the middle of the 70s had staked his claim to be one of the best defenders in the world. He was strong, fast, merciless in the tackle, skilful with his ball control, and a great reader of the game. In 1974 he was diagnosed with diabetes, but continued to play, keeping the condition under control with medication. He also suffered a fractured jaw and a mysterious foot ailment. He is considered to be one of the greatest players at Celtic, and in Scotland, and has been described as a player who probably "... had no superiors anywhere in the world".

McGrain made 659 appearances for Celtic, and helped them win the Scottish League Championship eight times, the Scottish Cup five times and the Scottish League Cup twice. He was Scottish Football Writers' Player of the Year in 1976-77. He was capped for Scotland 62 times

McGrain was given a free transfer by Celtic in May 1987 and then joined Hamilton Academicals.

In 1997 McGrain returned to Celtic and eventually became first-team coach.

McGrain has three daughters with his wife Laraine.

ĽUBOMÍR MORAVCÍK

Ľubomír "Lubo" Moravčík was born on the 22nd of June 1965 in Nitra, Czechoslovakia.

Moravčík joined Celtic in 1998 from German side MSV Duisburg, making 94 appearances until his departure in 2002. He became a star at Celtic Park, forming a formidable partnership with Henrik Larsson. Moravčík played in midfield, and became known for his technical skill and for his ability to use both feet when making accurate crosses and taking powerful shots at goal.

He gained 42 caps for the Czechoslovakian national side and 38 caps for the Slovakian national team. At Celtic, he won two Scottish League Championships, and one Scottish Cup.

Moravčík took up coaching in 2004.

BILLY MCNEILL

William "Billy" McNeill, was born on the 2nd of March 1940 in Bellshill, North Lanarkshire, Scotland.

McNeill joined Celtic in 1957 and stayed with the club until 1975 by which time he had made 790 appearances for the club without having been substituted once. He won nine Scottish League Championships, seven Scottish Cups and six Scottish League Cups with Celtic, also leading them to a European Cup victory in 1967. He also won 29 caps for Scotland. McNeill was voted Scottish Footballer of the Year for the 1964-65 season.

He displayed strong determination on the pitch to match his football talents, whilst his organisational abilities and good communication skills meant that he was soon appointed captain of the Celtic team.

McNeill moved to Clyde in April 1977 and into management before returning to Celtic in 1978 as their manager. After five years, Celtic had won three League Championships, one Scottish Cup and one League Cup. He left Celtic again in 1983 to manage Manchester City. In 1987, he returned to Celtic again, resigning after four years as manager in 1991. He helped the club to win the League/Scottish Cup Double in 1987-88 and the Scottish Cup in 1988-89.

Described as "a wonderful player and person", McNeill has been awarded an MBE, and his place in Celtic's book of honour is assured.

JIMMY MCGRORY

James Edward "Jimmy" McGrory was born on the 26th of April 1904 in Garngad, Glasgow, and died on the 20th of October 1982.

McGrory's parents were Irish Catholic immigrants from County Donegal. His father was a gas works labourer. McGrory signed for Celtic in June 1922 and made his debut on the 20th of January 1923. He became known as the "Human Torpedo" for his spectacular heading skills when he was almost horizontal in the air, and soon established himself as one of the most skillful and physically powerful forwards in the game, with the ability to score from any angle and any position.

McGrory holds the record for all-time leading goal scorer in the top echelons of British football, having scored 485 goals, plus 53 goals in secondary cup competitions, 6 goals for the Scottish national side and 6 for the Scottish League XI. He played for Celtic for 15 years from 1922 until 1937. Whilst there, he scored 469 goals in 448 games; he scored 57 League and Scottish Cup goals in 39 games in the 1926-27 season and holds the club's record for most goals in one season. It remains a bone of contention to this day that he was only given seven caps by the Scottish national team.

When he left Celtic, McGrory joined Kilmarnock as their manager, but returned in 1945 to take over the manager's position at Celtic, which he held for nearly twenty years. He presided over the momentous 1957 Scottish League Cup Final in which Celtic hammered Rangers 7-1, the greatest margin of victory ever in a British cup final and a record that holds to this day. Under his guidance, Celtic won the Scottish League Championship in 1953-54, the Scottish FA Cup in 1950-51 and 1953-54, and the Scottish League Cup in 1956-57 and 1957-58.

Jimmy McGrory was arguably the greatest Celtic man of all.

BOBBY LENNOX

Robert "Bobby" Lennox, was born on the 30th of August 1943 in Saltcoats, Ayrshire.

Lennox signed for Celtic on provisional forms of the age of 18 in 1961 and became a prolific goal scorer, second only to Jimmy McGrory. His exceptional speed was legendary and earned him the nickname, "Buzz Bomb". He played for the club from 1961 until 1978, and in those years he scored 273 goals from a total of 468 appearances. He was a member of the famous "Lisbon Lions", who won the European Cup in 1967. He also won 11 Scottish League medals, 8 Scottish Cup medals and 5 Scottish League Cup medals.

In March 1978, he left Celtic to play in America, but was recalled in September of the same year. In 1980 he retired, and became part of Celtic's coaching staff until 1981.

Bobby Charlton described Lennox as, "... one of the best strikers I have ever seen".

Lennox was awarded an MBE in 1981, and in November 2005 he was inducted into the Scottish Football Hall of Fame.

PAUL LAMBERT

Paul Lambert was born on the 7th of August 1969 in Paisley, Scotland, and won his first honours as a player at the age of 17, winning the Scottish Cup with St Mirren.

Lambert joined Celtic in November 1997 from German club Borussia Dortmund, and became a mainstay of the Celtic team. He won the Scottish Premier League 4 Times, the Scottish Cup 3 times, the Scottish League Cup twice, and was Scottish Football Writers' Player of the Year in 2002. In 2009 he was inducted into the Scottish Football Hall of Fame. Known for his leadership and combative playing abilities, Lambert became one of Celtic's best midfield players. He won forty caps for the Scottish national side.

After retiring as a player, Lambert turned to management, and having studied for football coaching qualifications in 2005, he has managed several English teams, the most prominent of which was Aston Villa.

SCOTT BROWN

Scott Brown was born on the 25th of June 1985 in Dunfermiline, Scotland. Scott was a schoolboy at Dalgety Bay Primary School, Hill of Beath Primary School (the same village in which the legendary Jim Baxter was born) and Beath High School.

At 13 he joined Hibernian, after Rangers had decided he was too small to be of use to them. He signed for Hibernian in 2002 as a midfielder and stayed with the club until 2007. After that, he came to Celtic, where he was to put in 407 appearances until departing for Aberdeen in 2021. He was handed the captaincy in 2010 and also captained the Scottish national squad for whom he was capped 55 times.

Brown joined Aberdeen in 2021 and retired from the game in May 2022, after 787 appearances for Hibernian, Celtic and Aberdeen. He has since taken up football management positions.

Scott and Lisa Taylor married in 2009 and they have three children, Sonny, Kit and Shay.

Renowned for his fierce tackling and relentless focus, Brown was often the recipient of yellow cards but was a powerhouse in the centre of the Celtic field and could be found anywhere between the boxes. One of his less admirable qualities was his mocking of opposition players. But his abilities were in no doubt, as he was a superb midfielder, holding the ball, reading the game and moving the play forward with sharp passes but also able to take the ball back into possession when needed, taking no prisoners whilst he did so.

SCOTT BROWN AWARDS:

- PFA Scotland Team of the Year, 2006–07, 2008–09, 2014–15, 2016–17, 2017–18, 2018–19
- SFW Young Player of the Year, 2006–07
- PFA Scotland Players' Player of the Year, 2008–09, 2017–18
- SFWA Footballer of the Year, 2017–18
- Scotland National Football Team Role of Honour, 2016

MOUSSA DEMBÉLÉ

Moussa Dembélé was born on the 12th of July 1996 in Pontoise, France.

His career started with the youth team of US Cergy Clos before he moved to Paris St Germain in 2004. His first move to the UK came when he joined Fulham, where he stayed until 2016.

The striker began his reign at Celtic that same year and would spend two years at the club making 55 appearances and taking 26 goals.

His career was interrupted by injury in the 2017-18 season, but nonetheless, Neil Lennon said of Moussa: "He is hugely important ... an outstanding footballer, almost talismanic ...He is up there with some of the best we've had over the last 20 years". Moussa was top goalscorer for three consecutive seasons.

MOUSSA DEMBÉLÉ AWARDS:

- London Football League Player of the Year, 2015-16
- Trophée Téléfoot du meilleur espoir français de l'année (France Under-21 Player of the Year), 2016
- Scottish Premiership Player of the Month: September 2016, February 2017
- PFA Scotland Team of the Year (Premiership), 2016-17
- PFA Scotland Goal of the Season, 2016-17
- Celtic Top Goalscorer, 2016-17
- Celtic Goal of the Season, 2016-17

JAMES FORREST

James Forrest was born on the 7th of July 1991 in Prestwick, Scotland.

Forrest started his football life with the South Ayr Boys Club before he caught the attention of Jim Began, Celtic's talent spotter. James was 11 years old and was attracting a lot of interest from other clubs, too. Aged just 13, he signed for Celtic on a youth contract and honed his obvious talent at Celtic's Hamilton coaching school. His first team career began in August 2009 and his first match came in May the following year.

Since 2011, the 5ft 7in-tall winger has been in the Scottish national team, and to the present date has made 275 appearances for Celtic scoring 62 goals.

Forrest is noted for his dynamic bursts of speed and high octane performances. He can pick up and hold the ball at speed over long distances, possessing as he does excellent ball control and dribbling abilities, which he can pair with wonderful finishing. He is also very good at reading the game and never shirks from being in difficult situations. He will never, as one player described it, avoid responsibility and can always be relied upon to deliver thrilling football for the fans.

JAMES FORREST AWARDS:

- SFWA Footballer of the Year, 2018–19
- PFA Scotland Players' Player of the Year, 2018–19
- SFWA Young Player of the Year, 2011–12
- PFA Scotland Team of the Year, 2011–12, 2017–18, 2018–19
- Scottish Premiership Player of the Year, 2018–19
- Scottish Premiership Player of the Month, October 2018
- SFWA International Player of the Year, 2018–19
- Celtic Young Player of the Year, 2010–11, 2011–12

ODSONNE ÉDOUARD

Odsonne Édouard was born on the 16th of January 1998 in Kourou, French Guiana.

He began playing with amateur side AF Bobigny, before taking up an offer to join the Paris Saint-Germain Academy in 2011. He was part of the Paris Saint-Germain B team for the 2015-16 season, and his chance for first-team experience came in the 2016-17 season.

Édouard came to Celtic on loan in 2017 but stayed with the club until 2021 having made 94 appearances and scoring 57 goals.

At 6ft 1in tall, Odsonne is a fast and powerful player who can finish a run into the opposition half with on-target shots at goal. His height makes him a useful player for high crosses. He never loses sight of the goal from wherever he is on the field, moving to wherever he is needed, slowing the game if need be and using his dribbling skills to bring the ball forward.

ODSONNE ÉDOUARD AWARDS:

- SFWA Footballer of the Year, 2019-20
- PFA Scotland Team of the Year, 2020-21 Scottish Premiership
- Scottish Premiership Top Scorer, 2019-20, 20 20-21
- Scottish Premiership Player of the Month, March 2019, August 2019, January 2020, February 2021
- UEFA European under 17 Championship Golden Player, 2015
- UEFA European under 17 Championship Top Scorer, 2015
- UEFA European under 17 Championship Team of the Tournament, 2015
- Titi d'Or, 2015
- Celtic Player of the Year, 2019-20

THE MANAGERS

A brief list of Celtic managers

WILLIE MALEY

William Patrick "Willie" Maley was born on the 25th of April 1868 in Newry, County Down, Northern Ireland and died on the 2nd of April 1958 in Glasgow.

Maley was born in the British Army barracks in Newry. His father was a soldier, and the family moved to Scotland when Maley was just a young boy.

He was signed by Celtic, then a new club, as a midfielder in 1888 and stayed with the club until 1897 making 75 appearances. He was not, by all accounts, one of the most sparkling players in the club. Nonetheless, he won 2 caps for Scotland.

Maley was just 29 years old in 1897, when the club's board of directors appointed him to be Secretary-Manager, in effect Celtic's first manager.

Maley's style was very different from today's hands-on managers; he was never involved in training the players, or in giving them morale-boosting talks; he was an authority figure, almost dictatorial, but a man who cared deeply about his players, nonetheless. He worked tirelessly for the good of the club, and changed its policy of buying professionals. He began to rely almost entirely on youngsters brought through from the junior teams. Thus he had a continuous pool of talent at his disposal for very little cost from which he constantly renewed his aging teams. In this way, he produced a team that won 6 consecutive league titles from 1905 to 1910, and won the first Scottish League and Scottish Cup Doubles. His 6 in-a-row record held until the 1960s. He also set a record for an unbeaten run of games in professional football; 62, of which 13 were drawn and 49 won between the 13th of November 1915 and the 21st of April 1917.

Maley's term as manager was the longest in Celtic's history, 43 years, and his pride in the club and the ethical compass he set still permeate the club today. During that time he won 19 Glasgow Charity Cups, 14 Glasgow Cups, 14 Scottish Cups, and 16 Scottish First Division Titles. Willie Maley was inducted into the Scottish Football Hall of Fame on the 15th of November 2009.

WILLIE MALEY

JIMMY MCGRORY

JIMMY MCGRORY

James Edward "Jimmy" McGrory was born on the 26th of April 1904 in Garngad, Glasgow, Scotland, and died on the 20th of October 1982 in Glasgow.

McGrory was the son of Irish Catholic immigrants from County Donegal, and when the family moved to Scotland, his father became a gas works labourer.

At the age of 16, McGrory began playing professional football for St. Roch's Juniors.

With his reputation growing, and many clubs wanting to acquire his talents, he signed for Celtic on the 10th of June 1922. His debut came on the 20th of January 1923. His insatiable appetite for goals was soon evident, and McGrory's strong physique was soon feared by the opposition as he thundered through the defences in search of goals.

In 1937 he left Celtic, having scored 469 goals in 448 games, and moved on to Clydebank.

In 1945 he returned to Celtic as their manager, a position he held for almost 20 years until he was succeeded by Jock Stein in 1965. This was a difficult period for Celtic – at one point they were almost relegated – a period during which McGrory was given hardly any power to make decisions by a board dominated by Bob Kelly. This did not help his authority amongst the players, whose behaviour towards him and others in his staff left much to be desired. He was a popular figure at Celtic, nonetheless.

McGrory presided over one of the most spectacular Old Firm results in Celtic history, when they hammered Rangers 7-1 in the Scottish League Cup final in 1957. Although this era was not a high point in Celtic's history, McGrory won the Scottish League Championship in 1953-54, the Scottish FA Cup in 1950-51 and 1953-54, and the Scottish League Cup in 1956-57 and 1957-58.

JOCK STEIN

John "Jock" Stein was born on the 5th of October 1922 in Burnbank, South Lanarkshire, Scotland, and died on the 10th of September 1985 in Cardiff, Wales.

After he left Greenfield School in 1937, Stein became a miner, and began playing for Blantyre Victoria in 1940. He then played for Albion Rovers where he stayed until 1950.

In 1946 Stein married Jeanie McCauley, and they had a son, George, and a daughter, Rosie. Jock and Jeannie stayed together until his death; she died at the age of 80, in August 2007.

Stein went to Wales to play for Llanelli, but missing Scotland he decided to return, and in 1951 he was signed as a reserve by Celtic.

A recurring ankle injury forced him to retire as a player in January 1957, and he took up the job of coach to the Celtic reserve team. In 1960 he went to Dunfermline Athletic as their manager, and came back to Celtic in 1965 to take over the

JOCK STEIN

manager's job there, the first Protestant to do so.

In 1967, Stein guided Celtic to victory in the 1967 European Cup Final against Internazionale, 2-1, the first time a Scottish, indeed a British club had won the trophy. Stein was awarded a CBE in 1970.

Stein's success continued into the 1970s, and Celtic created a record with 9 consecutive Scottish League championships. In 1973, Stein suffered a heart attack and in 1975 he was almost killed in a car crash in which he sustained severe injuries. When he returned for the 1976-77 season, he was unable to create the same success, and he was finally persuaded to give up his position in 1978.

After a brief spell with Leeds United, he became manager of the Scottish national side until 1985. On the 10th of September, following a game between Wales and Scotland, Stein collapsed, and it was thought that he had suffered a heart attack. He died not long afterwards - from a build up of fluid on his lungs. He was 62 years old.

Stein was inducted into the Scottish Sports Hall of Fame, and the Scottish Football Hall of Fame. He has also been voted the greatest ever Scottish manager, and Celtic fans voted him the greatest ever Celtic manager. A life size bronze statue of him stands outside Celtic Park.

Stein was undoubtedly one of Britain's greatest football managers, and he made his presence felt before he even took over at Celtic, insisting that he take decisions that concerned the team and not chairman Bob Kelly. When Celtic won the Scottish Cup final in 1965, the end of seven seasons without a trophy, the board was won over, and Stein could begin to form the team that he wanted. It was the start of a phenomenal career spanning thirteen years at Celtic, during which time Stein won the European Cup, 6 Scottish League Cups, and ten Scottish league championships.

Stein's management style was new at the club; he began to train the players himself and introduced innovative playing methods, after methodically analysing the run of play in matches. He encouraged players to test their own abilities on the field and to make more use of the space around them. He is also acknowledged by the men who played for him, to have been a father figure to the teams. One of his great skills as a manager was to encourage talented young players, and some of those who flourished under his guidance were Kenny Dalglish, Lou Macari, George Connelly, and Davie Hay.

Stein reached the zenith of his career during the 1966-67 season. Celtic became unstoppable in every competition they entered, winning the Scottish League Championship, the Scottish FA Cup, The Scottish League Cup, and most exciting of all, the European Cup. Bill Shankly, the immortal Liverpool manager, was moved to say, "Jock, you're immortal now!" He was indeed, and it was not only his managerial skill that made him so, but his humanity and respect for others. His lack of bigotry was a lesson to all when hatred was rife between Catholic and Protestant segments of the population in Scotland, shown by the fact that he lost friends once he joined Celtic.

Stein will be remembered forever as a uniquely talented giant of the football world.

BILLY MCNEILL

William "Billy" McNeill was born on the 2nd of March 1940 in Bellshill, Scotland.

McNeill began his management career at Clyde and Aberdeen before joining Celtic in 1978, where he stayed for five years, guiding the club to the League Championship and Scottish Cup Double in his first year. By the time he left at the end of the 1982-83 season, Celtic had won three league titles.

It was a difficult challenge, taking over from the legendary Jock Stein and trying to revive a team that was in the doldrums. There was little financial support available to build a team, and McNeill spent far too much time arguing his case with the Board of Directors. When the talented Charlie Nicholas was lost to Arsenal, disagreements between Billy McNeill and chairman Desmond White became public. McNeill finally left at the end 1982-83 season to take charge of Manchester City.

He was back in 1987, taking charge in Celtic's Centenary season, and once more led the club to glory. Celtic won the Double of the Scottish League Championship, and the Scottish FA Cup. The following year there was more success when Celtic won the Scottish FA Cup at the expense of Rangers, 1-0.

But behind the scenes, McNeill was still struggling to keep his best players from being sold by the board, who refused to release money for him to improve the team, and when poor results brought two seasons with no trophies, the man known as "Caesar", left Celtic.

In 2008, he was awarded an honorary degree from the University of Glasgow. In 2009 he became the club's ambassador.

BILLY MCNEILL

MARTIN O'NEILL

Martin Hugh Michael O'Neill, was born on the 1st of March 1952 in Kilrea, Northern Ireland. He was one of 9 children.

O'Neill became a football manager in 1987, and joined Celtic in the year 2000 after a decade in which the Glasgow club had struggled to bring home trophies. Success came immediately, and he presided over Celtic's domestic treble in his first season, the only manager since Jock Stein to have done so. In the 2001-02 season, O'Neill helped Celtic to retain the league title, the first time they had done so since 1982. The 2002-03 season proved to be a barren one, but the following season, O'Neill brought in the domestic double of the League Championship and the Scottish FA Cup. In the 2004-05 season, Celtic won the Scottish FA Cup once again. O'Neill then resigned as manager to look after his wife Geraldine who was suffering from lymphoma.

He returned to management in 2006, and took over the Republic of Ireland national team in 2013.

During his five-year tenure at Celtic, O'Neill revitalised the team, and guided them to a British record of 25 consecutive league victories, 3 league titles, 3 Scottish Cups, and one League Cup, as well as 7 consecutive victories in Old Firm derbies.
In 2004, O'Neill was awarded an OBE. He has also been voted Premier League Manager of the month 10 times, and Scottish Premier League Manager of the month 9 times. He was SFWA Manager of the Year for 3 years in a row.

O'Neill has two daughters with his wife Geraldine.

MARTIN O'NEILL

GORDON STRACHAN

Gordon David Strachan was born on the 9th of February 1957 in Edinburgh, Scotland.

Strachan's father worked as a scaffolder. The young Gordon began his football career at the age of 14 with Dundee, but damaged his eye in a football accident at the age of 15.

Strachan began his management career in 1996 at Coventry City, arriving at Celtic in 2005, where he was to stay for the next four years winning at least one trophy in each of those years. In his first season, which got off to a difficult start when Celtic lost 5-0 to Slovakian champions Artmedia Bratislava on the 27th of July 2005, Strachan helped the club win the Scottish League Cup and the Scottish Premier League title, which Celtic did in record time, having six matches still to play. The following year, Celtic retained the league title and won the Scottish FA Cup. They retained the league title for the third time in the 2007-08 season. In the 2008-09 season they just missed out on the league title, but won the Scottish League Cup.

GORDON STRACHAN

Despite his successes, Strachan's time at Celtic is generally not seen in a positive light by Celtic fans, as the quality of football was considered to be poor, even though he was well-liked by the players.

He was voted SPL Manager of the Year twice and SPF a Manager of the Year three times.

NEIL LENNON

Neil Lennon was born on the 25th of June 1971 in Lurgan, Northern Ireland, Where he was a pupil at St. Michael's grammar school. He began his professional career in 1986 with Glenavon, and joined Celtic in the year 2000 making 214 league appearances for the team until he left in 2007. He returned to Celtic in 2010 as caretaker manager, taking over on a full-time basis on the 9th of June.

Lennon brought home silverware in all of the seasons as manager at Celtic; he won the Scottish FA Cup in his first season; the following season Celtic won the Scottish Premier League Championship and in 2012-13 they won the Double of Scottish League Championship and Scottish FA Cup. In 2014 they won the Scottish Premiership for the third successive time under his management.

Lennon has been subjected to physical attacks and death threats as manager of Celtic; in 2011 he was sent several packages, one containing bullets, and others containing parcel bombs.

Lennon became SPL manager of the month 8 times, SPL Manager of the Year in 2011-12, SPFL Premiership Manager of the Month twice, and SFWA Manager of the Year twice. Criticised for not updating his tactics often enough, Lennon was, nevertheless, one of Celtic's most successful managers. He left Celtic in May 2014.

NEIL LENNON

RONNY DEILA

Ronny Deila was born on the 21st of September 1975 in Porsgrunn in southern Norway and - his mother wasn't sure he would make the grade as a pro footballer - trained as teacher before turning to football as a career.

His playing career began as a defender in 1992 with Uraedd, his local club, but he wasn't long with them before he was the target of attention from Odd Grenland, a club playing in the top Norwegian division. He moved to join them in 1993 soon becoming a pivotal part of their defensive lineup. He stayed with them until 2004, by which time he had notched up 240 appearances for them and scored 22 goals.

In his role as a defender, Deila was capped nine times with the Norwegian under-17 squad between 1992 and 1993, and in 1994 he appeared for the Norwegian under-18 team. He also made two appearances in 1996 for the under-21 team on a tour in the USA.

Leaving Odd, he moved first to Viking (2004-2005), and followed that with a short stay in 2005 as coach at Brodd in the Norwegian Fourth Division. He then went to Strømsgodset (2006-2008) where he was a player assistant and coach. There he took over from head coach Dag-Eilev Fagermo in 2007. Deila put away his playing boots when he was appointed manager.

He did, however, play on a part-time basis for Sparta/Bragerøen (2009-2011).

In 2013, Deila's coaching style - he is known for favouring an attacking style of football - was rewarded with the Kinksen Award for Coach of the Year.

He stayed as manager of Strømsgodset until 2014 putting great emphasis on the development of players and of himself. He visited several European clubs, such as German side Dortmund, studying coaching and training methods and honing his understanding of the best tactics.

He was invited to take up the reins at Celtic on the 6th June 2014 on a 12-month rolling contract, an appointment he described as "a magnificent honour".

Deila is quoted as saying, "Until I win something I will be questioned. That just motivates me and I have one goal – to win everything in Scotland", and he has certainly pursued that goal with clarity and determination, winning both the Scottish League Cup and the Scottish League Premiership in 2015.

Deila has two twin teenage daughters, who have stayed behind in Norway with his wife, part of the sacrifice that managing a top club can bring in its wake.

He has strong opinions, which is almost a contractual clause for any top-flight manager these days, but he combines his confidence with humour and an understanding of people. When defender Dedryck Boyata signed from Manchester City, Deila invited the player to live with him, treating him "like a son", in the player's own words. This protective characteristic in the manager bodes well for the future. Deila has been described as tough but fair, which is what any player will want in a manager. "When you put the Celtic shirt on you must give 100 per cent", he says.

Everyone at Celtic will heartily agree with that.

BRENDAN RODGERS

Brendan Rodgers was born on the 26th of January 1973 in Carnlough, Northern Ireland. He lost his parents before they reached their sixtieth year and they died within one year of each other aged 53 and 59. Rodgers has two children with his wife Susan, from whom he is separated; Anton and Mischa.

The eldest of five boys, Rodgers attended All Saints Catholic Primary School and then St. Patrick's College and played for Northern Ireland at schoolboy level.

Playing as a defender, his professional debut came in 1987 for Ballymena United, and he then moved to Reading in England. However, a knee condition forced him to retire from playing at the age of 20. After this, he took a position as a coach with Reading, then becoming Academy Director, whilst continuing to play non-league football with Newport, Witney Town and Newbury Town. He travelled around Spain studying coaching methods. Rodgers is known for his excellent man-to-man management style and desire to keep the game flowing forwards. He was then asked by José Mourinho to become youth manager at Chelsea. That was in 2004, and he became reserve manager in 2006.

Watford was his next move where, as manager, he managed to keep the team from relegation but left after one season, and having joined Reading, he departed after just six months when the results were far from satisfactory.

A stint at Swansea then found him in charge at Liverpool, where he kept the team in the top ten in his first season and then, in the 2012/13 season, he became the first Liverpool manager to win the LMA Manager of The Year Award. Liverpool came 6th the following season and were without any silverware. The directors were expecting more and Rodgers was unceremoniously sacked in October 2015.

Rodgers then came to Celtic on the 20th of May 2016, with a contract on a 12-month rolling basis. It's hardly surprising that after such a debut season his contract was extended.
Speaking two foreign languages (Italian and Spanish) and revelling in the nickname 'Buck Rodgers', the manager is a firm believer in maintaining possession of the ball with swift passing and pressurising opponents when they have the ball.

He won numerous trophies with Celtic including the Scottish Cup in May 2017 and the Scottish League Cup in 2018 Rodgers seventh successive trophy with the club. He departed for Leicester City in February 2019.

BRENDAN RODGERS AWARDS.

- LMA Manager of the Year 2013/14.
- PFA Scotland Manager of the Year 2016/17.
- Premier League Manager of the Month, January 2012, August 2013, March 2014.
- Football League Championship Manager of the Month, February 2011.
- Scottish Premiership Manager of the Month, August 2016, October 2016, December 2016, April 2017.
- SFWA Manager of the Year 2017.

ANGELOS POSTECOGLOU

Angelos Postecoglou was born on the 27th of August 1965 in Nea Filadelfeia, Greece.

In 1970, when Angelos was five years old, his family emigrated to Australia where the young boy grew up in Melbourne. At the age of nine, he joined South Melbourne Club and played for them, the Western Suburbs and the Australian national senior teams as a defender until a knee injury ended his career.

His new career as a team manager began in 1996, again with the South Melbourne club. After managing a variety of Australian clubs, he moved to Japan, arriving in Scotland to manage Celtic in 2021.

When he took over the club, as the first Australian to coach a major league European club, they were coming out of an unsuccessful season with no silverware, but by the end of his first season in charge, Celtic had won a domestic double having claimed the Scottish Premiership and the Scottish League Cup.

Angelos Postecoglou's first Old Firm success came in February 2022, when Celtic beat Rangers at Celtic Park 3-0. The league was sealed on the 11 May with a game remaining. Postecoglou became the first Australian to win a league title in Europe. He has won the PFA Scotland Manager of the Year and the SFWW Manager of the Year.

Angelos Postecoglou is married to Georgia with whom he has three sons.

THE STATISTICS

POSITION IN THE LEAGUE:

SCOTTISH FOOTBALL LEAGUE

1890-91 - 3
1891/92 - 2
1892/93 - 1
1893/94 - 1
1894/95 - 2
1895/96 - 1
1896/97 - 4
1897/98 - 1
1898/99 - 3
1899/1900 - 2
1900/01 - 2
1901/02 - 2
1902/03 - 5
1903/04 - 4
1904/05 - 1
1905/06 - 1
1906/07 - 1
1907/08 - 1
1908/09 - 1
1909/10 - 1
1910/11 - 5
1911/12 - 2
1912/13 - 1
1913/14 - 1
1914/15 - 1

FIRST WORLD WAR

1919/20 - 2
1920/21 - 2
1921/22 - 1
1922/23 - 3
1923/24 - 3
1924/25 - 4
1925/26 - 1
1926/27 - 3
1927/28 - 1
1928/29 - 2
1929/30 - 4
1930/31 - 2
1931/32 - 3
1932/33 - 4
1933/34 - 3
1934/35 - 2
1935/36 - 1
1936/37 - 3
1937/38 - 1
1938/39 - 2

WORLD WAR TWO

1946/47 - 7
1947/48 - 12
1948/49 - 6
1949/50 - 5
1950/51 - 7
1951/52 - 9
1952/53 - 8
1953/54 - 1
1954/55 - 2
1955/56 - 5
1956/57 - 5
1957/58 - 3
1958/59 - 6
1959/60 - 9
1960/61 - 4
1961/62 - 3
1962/63 - 4
1963/64 - 3
1964/65 - 8
1965/66 - 1
1966/67 - 1
1967/68 - 1
1968/69 - 1
1969/70 - 1
1970/71 - 1
1971/72 - 1
1972/73 - 1
1973/74 - 1
1974/75 - 3

SCOTTISH PREMIER DIVISION

1975/76 - 2
1976/77 - 1
1977/78 - 1
1978/79 - 1
1979/80 - 2
1980/81 - 1
1981/82 - 1
1982/83 - 2
1983/84 - 2
1984/85 - 2
1985/86 - 1
1986/87 - 2
1987/88 - 1
1988/89 - 3
1989/90 - 5
1990/91 - 3
1991/92 - 3
1992/93 - 3
1993/94 - 2
1994/95 - 2
1995/96 - 1
1996/97 - 2
1997/98 - 1

SCOTTISH PREMIER LEAGUE

1998/99 - 2
1999/2000 - 2
2000/01 - 1
2001/02 - 1
2002/03 - 2
2003/04 - 1
2004/05 - 2
2005/06 - 1
2006/07 - 1
2007/08 - 1
2008/09 - 2
2009/10 - 2
2010/11 - 2
2011/12 - 1
2012/13 - 2

SCOTTISH PREMIERSHIP

2013/14 - 1
2013/14 - 1
2014/15 - 1
2015/16 - 1
2016/17 - 1
2017/18 -1
2018/19 -1
2019/20 -1
2020/21 -2
2021/22 -1

CUP COMPETITIONS:

EUROPEAN CUP:

1967 - Celtic 2-1 Internazionale

GLASGOW CUP:

1891 - Celtic 4-0 Third Lanark
1892 - Celtic 7-1 Clyde
1895 - Celtic 2-0 Rangers
1896 - Celtic 6-3 Queen's Park
1905 - Celtic 2-1 Rangers
1906 - Celtic 3-0 Third Lanark
1907 - Celtic 3-2 Third Lanark
1908 - Celtic 2-2 Rangers
1908 - Celtic 0-0 Rangers (replay)
1908 - Celtic 2-1 Rangers (2nd replay)
1910 - Celtic 1-0 Rangers
1916 - Celtic 2-1 Rangers
1917 - Celtic 3-1 Clyde
1920 - Celtic 1-0 Partick Thistle
1921 - Celtic 1-0 Clyde
1927 - Celtic 1-0 Rangers
1928 - Celtic 2-0 Rangers
1929 - Celtic 2-0 Queen's Park
1931 - Celtic 2-1 Rangers
1939 - Celtic 3-0 Clyde

CUP COMPETITIONS:

1941 - Celtic 1-0 Rangers
1949 - Celtic 3-1 Third Lanark
1956 - Celtic 1-1 Rangers
1956 - Celtic 5-3 Rangers (replay)
1962 - Celtic 1-1 Third Lanark
1962 - Celtic 3-2 Third Lanark (replay)
1964 - Celtic 2-0 Clyde
1965 - Celtic 5-0 Queen's Park
1967 - Celtic 4-0 Partick Thistle
1968 - Celtic 8-0 Clyde
1970 - Celtic 3-1 Rangers
1975 - Celtic 2-2 Rangers (shared)
1982 - Celtic 2-1 Rangers
2008 - Celtic 3-1 Rangers
2011 - Celtic 1-0 Rangers
2014 - Celtic 1-0 Rangers

SCOTTISH LEAGUE CUP:

1956-57 Celtic 0-0 Partick Thistle
1956-57 Celtic 3-0 Partick Thistle (replay)
1957-58 Celtic 7-1 Rangers
1965-66 Celtic 2-1 Rangers
1966-67 Celtic 1-0 Rangers
1967-68 Celtic 5-3 Dundee
1968-69 Celtic 6-2 Hibernian
1969-70 Celtic 1-0 St. Johnstone
1974-75 Celtic 6-3 Hibernian
1982-83 Celtic 2-1 Rangers
1997-98 Celtic 3-0 Dundee United
1999-00 Celtic 2-0 Aberdeen
2000-01 Celtic 3-0 Kilmarnock
2005-06 Celtic 3-0 Dunfermline Athletic
2008-09 Celtic 2-0 Rangers
2014-15 Celtic 2 - 0 Dundee United
2016/17 - Celtic 3-0 Aberdeen
2017/18 - Celtic 2-0 Motherwell
2018/19 - Celtic 1-0 Aberdeen
2019/20 - Celtic 1-3 Rangers
2021/22 - Celtic 2-1 Hibernian

THE DRYBROUGH CUP:

1974 Celtic 2-2 Rangers (Celtic 4-2 on penalties)

THE GLASGOW MERCHANTS' CHARITY CUP:

1892 - Celtic 2-0 Rangers
1893 - Celtic 5-0 Rangers
1894 - Celtic 2-1 Queen's Park
1895 - Celtic 4-0 Rangers
1896 - Celtic 2-1 Queen's Park
1899 - Celtic 2-0 Rangers
1903 - Celtic 5-2 St. Mirren
1905 - Celtic 2-0 Partick Thistle
1908 - Celtic 3-0 Queen's Park
1912 - Celtic 0-0 Clyde (Celtic 7-2 on corners)
1913 - Celtic 3-2 Rangers
1914 - Celtic 6-0 Third Lanark
1915 - Celtic 3-2 Rangers
1916 - Celtic 2-0 Partick Thistle
1917 - Celtic 1-0 Queen's Park
1980 - Celtic 2-0 Partick Thistle
1920 - Celtic 1-0 Queen's Park
1921 - Celtic 2-0 Rangers
1924 - Celtic 2-1 Rangers
1926 - Celtic 2-1 Queen's Park
1936 - Celtic 4-2 Rangers
1937 - Celtic 4-3 Queen's Park
1938 - Celtic 2-0 Rangers
1934 - Celtic 3-0 Third Lanark
1943 - Celtic 3-1 Third Lanark
1950 - Celtic 3-2 Rangers
1953 - Celtic 3-1 Queen's Park
1959 - Celtic 5-0 Clyde
1961 - Celtic 1-1 Clyde (shared)

SCOTTISH FA CUP:

1891-92 Celtic 1-0 Queen's Park
1891-92 Celtic 5-1 Queen's Park (replay after protests)
1898-99 Celtic 2-0 Rangers
1899-1900 Celtic 4-3 Queen's Park
1903-04 Celtic 3-2 Rangers
1906-07 Celtic 3-0 Heart of Midlothian
1907-08 Celtic 5-1 St. Mirren
1910-11 Celtic 0-0 Hamilton Academical
1910-11 Celtic 2-0 Hamilton Academical (replay)
1911-12 Celtic 2-0 Clyde
1913-14 Celtic 0-0 Hibernian
1913-14 Celtic 4-1 Hibernian (replay)
1922-23 Celtic 1-0 Hibernian
1924-25 Celtic 2-1 Dundee
1926-27 Celtic 3-1 East Fife
1930-31 Celtic 2-2 Motherwell
1930-31 Celtic 4-2 Motherwell (replay)
1932-33 Celtic 1-0 Motherwell
1936-37 Celtic 2-1 Aberdeen
1950-51 Celtic 1-0 Motherwell
1953-54 Celtic 2-1 Aberdeen
1964-65 Celtic 3-2 Dunfermline Athletic
1966-67 Celtic 2-0 Aberdeen
1968-69 Celtic 4-0 Rangers
1970-71 Celtic 1-1 Rangers
1970-71 Celtic 2-1 Rangers (replay)
1971-72 Celtic 6-1 Hibernian
1973-74 Celtic 3-0 Dundee United
1974-75 Celtic 3-1 Airdrieonians
1976-77 Celtic 1-0 Rangers
1979-80 Celtic 1-0 Rangers
1984-85 Celtic 2-1 Dundee United
1987-88 Celtic 2-1 Dundee United
1988-89 Celtic 1-0 Rangers
1994-95 Celtic 1-0 Airdrieonians
2000-01 Celtic 3-0 Hibernian
2003-04 Celtic 3-1 Dunfermline Athletic
2004-05 Celtic 1-0 Dundee United
2006-07 Celtic 1-0 Dunfermline Athletic
2010-11 Celtic 3-0 Motherwell
2012-13 Celtic 3-0 Hibernian
2016/17 Celtic 2-1 Aberdeen
2017/18 - Celtic 2-0 Motherwell
2018/19 - Celtic 2-1 Heart of Midlothian
2019/20 - Celtic 3-3 Heart of Midlothian a.e.t (Celtic won 4-3 on penalties)

v. RANGERS
HAMPDEN PARK
Turnstile J
WEST TERRACING COVERED
10294
FINAL TIE
KILMARNOCK F.C. v CELTIC F.C.
THE NATIONAL STADIUM, HAMPDEN PARK, GLASGOW
SUNDAY 18TH MARCH 2001, KICK-OFF 3.00PM
SOUTH LOWER I
79-86
46
W
48
£17
U.E.F.A. - F.I.G.C.
MILANO - STADIO S. SIRO
FINALE COUPE DES CLUBS CHAMPIONS EUROPEENS
GRADINATE
33977
UEFA
J. KENNAWAY
EAST STAND
FUSSBALL-CLUB BASEL
Europa-Meister-Cup
Mittwoch, 17. September
Tribüne Parterre
Sektor
SEMI-FINAL TIE
CELTIC v. RANGERS
HAMPDEN PARK, GLASGOW
TUESDAY 31st MARCH, 1992
Kick-off 8.00 p.m.
Price £6·00
Turnstile P
JOCK STEIN TERRACING UNCOVERED
01955
SCOTTISH PREMIER LEAGUE
RANGERS v. CELTIC
IBROX STADIUM
SATURDAY 1st NOVEMBER, 1980
KICK-OFF 3.00 p.m.
£3.00
THIS PORTION TO BE RETAINED BY THE HOLDER
J.QUINN CELTIC F.C.
J. Campbell
OGDEN'S CIGARETTES
COUPE UEFA
1999/2000
32eme Finale - Match aller
OLYMPIQUE LYONNAIS
CELTIC GLASGOW
Stade de Gerland
COPA DEL MUNDO
1967
Sector "B"
1986
THE SKOL CUP
SPONSORED BY ALLOA BREWERY COMPANY
FINAL TIE
Celtic v. Rangers
HAMPDEN PARK, GLASGOW
SUNDAY, 26th OCTOBER, 1986
KICK-OFF 3.00 p.m.
TO BE RETAINED
SEMI-FI
HAMPDEN
WEDNESDAY
SOUTH EAST STAND
TURNSTILE B
PRICE £10
SMITH'S CIGARETTES
CELTIC.
КВИТОК
СЕКТОР
РЯД
МІСЦЕ
MANCHESTER UNITED
N LOWER
СЕЛТИК
ЦЕНА 15.
SCOTTISH FOOTBALL ASSOCIATION
TENNENTS SCOTTISH CUP
CELTIC v FALKIR
IBROX STADIUM, GLASGOW
MAIN REAR
SECTION MRC
ROW K
SEAT 86
SCOTTISH FOOTBALL ASSOCIATION
TENNENTS SCOTTISH CUP
SEMI-FINAL TIE
HIBERNIAN F.C. v. CELTIC F.C.
IBROX STADIUM, GLASGOW
Friday, 7th April, 1995 Kick-off 7.45pm
ENCLOSURE EAST
SECTION 3
ROW J
SEAT 90
PRICE £14
TO BE RETAINED - SEE BACK FOR PLAN AND CONDITIONS
IS INVALID UNLESS PRESENTED IN FULL
CELTIC
DIXIE DEANS
FORWARD
NGERS
EP 8 205
HONDA
CELTIC
ROY AITKEN
UEFA CHAMPIONS LEAGUE
CELTIC v AC MILAN
TUESDAY, 20 FEBRUARY 2007: 7:45PM
JOCK STEIN LOWER
T97,T101-T103 - GREEN
INTERNAZ
CELTIC
MARNOCK
FINAL